I0462074

The People's Constitution

(2018 Edition)

By John Andrews

For the 99%, with love...

Dear Reader,

There's good news and there's bad news. Let's get the bad news out of the way first: The world is in a mess... a very serious mess.

Now for the good news: we can fix it.

The specific purpose of this book is to show exactly how we could fix it, to provide a type of blueprint of a constitution for a government that could, and should in my view, be used by any country that aims to be a real democracy, one that's truly concerned with the wellbeing of its people, understands the vital importance of protecting all its wildlife, and is determined to preserve and maintain the health of its natural environment.

However, I must state clearly at the outset, that unless you, dear reader, are one of a growing number of well-enlightened people, you may struggle to understand the vital need for this book. That's because you may think this book is based on nonsense, or "Conspiracy Theories" perhaps. Unfortunately, however, it is not based on nonsense or conspiracy theories, it's based on truth and hard facts, and a growing number of well-enlightened people know that. If you are not yet well-enlightened, please read the companion book to this one called "The School of Kindness", where I outline many of the issues that people really need to know and *understand, as well as providing a sizeable source of verifiable information to support that claim.*

At the time of writing, it's true to say that very few people properly understand how bad things really are; and of those very few, some actually like it that way. Others, almost unbelievably, are trying to make matters even worse. But some of the very few who properly understand are appalled by the immensity of the problem, and we strive every day of our lives to fix it.

If you, dear reader, are one of the very few enlightened souls who already know how bad things really are, and also yearn to fix it; if you're already intimately familiar with the work of great torchbearers such as Pilger, Newsinger, Roy, Chomsky, Media Lens, Zinn, Klein, Blum... to name but a few, I hope you'll find this book thought-provoking, and possibly inspirational.

But unfortunately most people have never heard of Noam Chomsky, whose work is much respected by many of us around the world - let alone Naomi Klein say, or Bill Blum. Neither are they familiar with the powerful films, journalism and TV work of the likes of Michael Moore, John Pilger or Matt Taibbi, and don't understand the wonderful protest songs of the likes of the all-but-unknown genius Robb Johnson. Although many might vaguely recall the name Julian Assange and his fantastic Wikileaks project from our so-called "news", relatively few have actually seen it and grasped the enormous implications of it. As for some of the other great websites which provide truly useful information such as ZNet, Dissident Voice, Media Lens... and many others, these great information sources are all but unknown except to a tiny handful of us. So it's very difficult for those who do not know about the vast body of evidence these writers, artists, journalists and film-makers provide of the sheer evil of our trusted leaders to understand why that powerful and emotive word, "evil", is not an exaggeration when applied to our system of government, and therefore why work such as this book is so important.

Nothing better demonstrates and proves the incompetence, deceit and corruption of our trusted leaders than our planet's condition of Permanent War and its vital twin, the cynically manufactured and carefully maintained state of Permanent Fear. And nothing better illustrates the utter subjugation of humanity by these same trusted rulers than the inability of ordinary people to do very much about it.

This book is based on two core assumptions: that our leaders are not to be trusted, not any of them; and that the overwhelming majority of non-leaders (i.e. most of us) are good and decent people who, ***if given good information***, will make good and decent decisions - without needing any leaders at all.

Truth is a very elusive thing, especially where governments are concerned; and whilst I can't guarantee all *the information in these pages is absolutely truthful and correct, it's as honest and accurate as I can make it. However, I do not pretend to be unbiased. I am strongly biased - in favour of the vast majority of humanity who, through no fault of their own, are hugely deceived. I am biased in favour of the vast majority of people who want no more than to live and let live, to cause no harm, and to live happy lives with friends and family. As well as this vast majority of humanity my work is also strongly biased in favour of all other living things – and it is just as strongly biased against those who oppress and plunder and ruin our planet. I make no apology for this bias, and I do not try to hide it: we are bombarded twenty four hours a day with the distractions, misinformation and lies of our trusted leaders, just to serve the venal purposes of the 1%, so why not a little bias that supports the vast majority of humanity for a change?*

There are two main reasons why I've written this book. Firstly it angers me that so many people have been so horribly used in the past by people they not only trusted, but often worshipped too; and how good people continue to be deceived today in exactly the same way by an inhumane and utterly brutal system that has always valued elitist wealth above compassion for humanity and concern for other living things. Secondly I worry about the future: the children and young people I see around me; the unborn generations to come; the condition of this once beautiful fragile world, a planet being rapidly destroyed in the sacred name of 'MORE' – all to be left to the tender mercies of this same evil system. And do please believe me, dear reader, "evil" is not too strong a word to use for those who maintain this situation; for although I'm sure it was seldom a conscious intention to create an evil system, it is most certainly what has transpired.

Technology is improving every day. Often this is for the good, but it creates the illusion that society is improving too. It's a very dangerous illusion, because the way our society is controlled is essentially unchanged from the way it's always been: exploitation of the weak by a tiny minority of rich and powerful people. So although technology is indeed vastly improved, our governments still work in basically the same primitive way as they have always done: through deceit and oppression.

As I slowly uncover the way our world really works, slowly discover the vital facts that are so carefully kept just out of public view, I feel that if I don't try to pass on what I've learnt, and offer a real solution to fix the mess our world is in, then surely I will have failed the future – and that simply will not do. Because our lives are truly worthless unless they can somehow be turned to help those less fortunate or less knowing, I now feel I can look the future squarely in the eye, proudly show them this book, and say: "I tried."

Great Gonerby

May 2018

The People's Constitution

"Let it be heard and let man learn to feel that the true greatness of a nation is founded on principles of humanity."

Tom Paine
"Prospects on the Rubicon"

Contents

Foreword to the 2018 edition 1
Introduction to the People's Constitution 12
Proper Information 38
Welcome to the world of EnMo Economics 50
A Question of Conscience.. 56
Transition... 60
The People's Constitution 74
    Section 1.   **Purpose** 76
    Section 2.   **The Citizen and their Individual Rights**. 80
    Section 3.   **The Citizen and their Individual**
    Responsibilities 86
    Section 4.   **The Democratic Process** 88
    Section 5.   **The Organisation and Responsibilities of**
    the State   94
    Section 6 – *The Economy* 125
    Section 7 – The Press, Media and the Arts 149
    Section 8 – The Environment and Animal Welfare,
    National Heritage, Agriculture, Transport, Essential
    Services, Communications and Natural Resources. . 153
    Section 9 – Social Welfare 157
    Section 10 - International Relations 163
    Section 11 – States of Emergency 166
Addendum A 170
Ethical Guide... 170
Addendum B 176
Possible Voting Mechanism... 176
Addendum C 181
Organisation of Public Services 181

Foreword to the 2018 edition
(Them and Us)

"Man was born free,
And he is everywhere in chains."

Jean-Jacques Rousseau
'The Social Contract'

I have made several changes to the previous edition of this book. New alterations to the actual text of the Constitution itself are mostly quite minor, and done with the purpose of trying to clarify and tighten it, trying to leave less "wriggle-room" for those few who would inevitably try to destroy it for their own selfish purposes.

Them and Us

Although it isn't necessary to have read my book *"The School of Kindness"* before reading this one, it might help to do so; because that book provides the evidence for the core assumptions that underpin the Peoples' Constitution: that we the 99% are mostly good and decent people; and that the 1%, our great trusted leaders, cannot in fact be trusted. However, if, dear reader, you're lucky enough to already know that, and do not need me to prove it, you could easily read this work and think about it based on its content alone.

This book does not go into all of the arguments its contents could provoke; it's main purpose is to state a model for a much better type of government than the one we have - based on the assumption that our existing system of government is corrupt and wholly controlled by tiny groups of utterly ruthless individuals whose personal hubris, stupidity, selfishness and greed is such that their actions can only be described as evil; and that a system of government run by such people is obviously not fit for purpose and must be changed. This book does not prove that core assumption. It assumes, dear reader, that you, like many other fairly well-enlightened people, already know that.

On September 17th in 2011 a fantastic thing happened. The world improved very slightly with the birth of a new populist movement. Its first appearance on western TV screens came from the heart of the US banking industry, where protesters had filled the streets outside of some of the most important financial institutions on the planet. The movement became known as Occupy Wall Street.

This mass of people, quite well-enlightened people, perfectly identified the main cause of most of the world's woes: the western banking system. The Occupy Movement rapidly spread, firstly across the United States and then, as the cause resonated with hundreds of thousands of similar voices around the globe, it raced like wildfire across most of the First World reaching almost every major city and

2

countless towns. All over the western world people started gathering together in numbers ranging from mere handfuls to tens of thousands to express a common message, a common rage: the people had had enough of the global plundering, vandalism, oppression and death being perpetrated by a corrupt and unaccountable banking system.

Inevitably the movement was gradually suppressed - violently. Peaceful protesters, who were doing more good for the cause of normal people - for us, the 99% - than all of the west's politicians combined, were beaten-up, tazered, gassed, water-cannoned, pepper-sprayed and imprisoned by ruthless militarised police - some of whom clearly relished their work. The harmless, peaceful, thriving tent-cities of the protesters were demolished and swept up into garbage trucks – usually in the small hours of morning, which has always been the preferred time for police-states to carry out their work.

But although most of the fine people of the Occupy Movement went to ground to lick their wounds and re-group, they left behind them an indestructible legacy. Arguably the single most iconic image of the Occupy Movement was their depiction of the cold fact that the world is divided into two groups, two vastly disproportionate groups: the 99% and the 1%, Us and Them. They made clear that it's the 1% who not only own the vast majority of the planet's wealth, they also control the vast majority of the planet's political power. Of course there's nothing new about this situation, it's always been like that; but the Occupy Movement brought out this very obvious injustice into the glaring light of day and placed it front and centre of their cause. Ordinary people who hadn't previously thought about the injustice of it saw it for the first time and began to wonder, began to ask how something as boring as a banking system could be so evil.

The information that most people receive, upon which they form opinions and judgements about how our world works, is provided by education systems and mass media that are almost entirely controlled by the 1%. Government is run by the 1%. At the risk of stating the blindingly obvious, the 1% will not supply the evidence of their own wrongdoing – we must find the time, and make the effort, to look for it elsewhere.

Most so-called experts will not approve of my books – just as they do not approve of Chomsky, Pilger or Zinn - for example. But far from being deterred by the experts' disapproval the average reader should instead be much encouraged. At first glance that statement might seem counterintuitive, but the reason I make it is actually pretty obvious. It just requires a little thought.

Consider, the world is run by vast armies of eminent experts of one type or another... and look at the state of it. We have economic experts, political experts, scientific experts, media experts, legal experts... to name but a few; then of course we have the 1% themselves, various kings, queens, emperors, prime ministers and presidents, together with their armies of so-called "advisers" – who together qualify as experts of some kind – and we have mighty admirals, air marshals and generals – all experts in the highly complicated business of slaughtering defenceless people in industrial quantities. **All these hundreds of thousands of eminent experts... and look at the world they've created**:

We have a global economy owned and run by the 1%, for the 1%, at the same time as we have hundreds of millions of people living on the brink of starvation. We have human overpopulation and grotesque environmental vandalism that is currently causing the sixth mass extinction of species - the greatest global environmental catastrophe since dinosaurs disappeared. We have massive social injustice that oversees vast numbers of political prisoners being murdered, "disappeared", tortured and locked up without charge or trial for months and years on end; others of Us, the 99%, are trafficked as sex slaves or condemned to fragile lives on the brink of survival as refugees and asylum seekers which, according to a report by UNHCR in 2015 was equivalent to 1 in every 122 people... and all this before we consider the greatest manmade abomination of them all: Permanent War.

In truth, this particular abomination shouldn't be dignified with the word "war". War suggests brave people sometimes doing heroic things for the sake of the survival of their homelands. None of the actions in which western armies have involved themselves since the Second World War (and there have been many, many such actions) have been necessary for the safety of western homelands. Certainly nothing these armies have done this last half century and more was heroic. Hundreds of millions of people, most of whom were innocent defenceless civilians, have been killed, directly or indirectly, by western forces since 1945 (actions which have long been defined as war-crimes and or crimes against humanity).

Such is the state of the world that's been created by the 1% and their experts, and is carefully maintained in that condition by the 1% and their experts. So when I point out that this book will definitely not be welcomed by experts it isn't something that concerns me; I see the disapproval of experts as a validation of my work, a confirmation of its real worth, and a strong recommendation to the average reader who is, after all, for whom it's intended.

A vast and daily-growing gulf exists between the 1% and the 99% - Them and Us. The most obvious manifestation of it can be seen, on the one side, in the glitzy trappings of the super-rich: the luxurious gated communities and guarded mansions, the private tropical islands, the yachts, private jets and sports cars, the million dollar trinkets and baubles, the packed closets of wear-once-only shoes that cost thousands of dollars a pair. And on the other side we see the crushing poverty of the super-poor – the shanty towns, the refugee camps, the bare-foot pot-bellied children, the so-called "Enterprise Zones" where Third World slaves endure lives akin to battery chickens... the mass starvation. These examples are the obvious signs of the differences between Them and Us.

The less obvious signs of difference, but arguably even more important, is the difference in how justice is measured out. This can be seen when one of the 99% can be casually murdered or disappeared by the agents of the 1%, or instantly imprisoned for six months or more for stealing a bottle of water (Tottenham 2011), for example. But when members of the 1% steal billions of dollars, or perpetrate war crimes, they never even have to appear in court, let alone serve any jail time; and it can be seen even more clearly when the armed servants of the 1% beat up and imprison harmless protestors without penalty (or even gun down defenceless civilians in cold blood) comfortable in the knowledge their 1% masters will ensure they never see the inside of a courtroom to face justice for their actions.

Most of humanity exists somewhere in between the extremes, brainwashed from birth to idolise, dream of and lust after the lives of the super-rich - partly by being kept terrified of the reality of life for the super-poor.

There have been many attempts throughout history to eliminate the gulf between Them and Us. The popular revolutions of the seventeenth, eighteenth and nineteenth centuries were arguably the first major demonstrations in modern history of popular resistance to the power of the 1%. Arguably the most successful uprising was the emergence and spread of socialism in the nineteenth and twentieth centuries, reaching its zenith in the 1970s. However, ever since the 70's the tide turned and socialism has been in decline – not through any particular weakness of the model itself, but because of the crushing power of the 1%, its bitter enemies who were never sufficiently beaten.

The greatest weakness of socialism lies in its obsession with wealth rather than justice. Communism – the extreme form of socialism - argues that everyone should be equally wealthy. It is a mistaken concept. People do not need to be equally wealthy, but we do need equal justice. Providing that everyone has enough of everything they really need, in exchange for a modest amount of their labour, most people don't need very much more. That view is similar to socialism, which was demonstrably successful in countries where it had a chance to develop a little - such as in Scandinavia. But socialism never really provided well for those who wanted more, and there will always be those who want more. There's nothing wrong with that, and nothing wrong with people having more - providing those who want it also work more, and their work does not exploit or harm others, and doesn't cause irreparable harm to the environment.

Throughout history every empire that has come and gone has been modelled on Them and Us – the 1% and the 99%. The 99% have always tolerated this for two reasons: because they fear the consequences of opposition and resistance, or (and this is probably the majority of cases) because they believe a lie. That lie, inevitably, is peddled by the 1% and their lackeys, and that lie is this: the 1% will always use their considerable power selflessly, responsibly, and in the interests of the 99%. Evidence of the lie is easy to find, as I showed in *"School of Kindness"*; but it goes to the very heart of the main problem that has to be overcome - the fact that the 99% are conditioned to trust their leaders. **It is a very misplaced trust.** The *"School of Kindness"* project is dedicated to the task of properly educating the young about this issue, and re-educating the not-so-young.

The People's Constitution is a new and very different model of government. At its heart is justice - humane justice - justice for 100% of the people, as well as permanent protection for our planet's fragile life-sustaining environment. It suggests a system of political decision-making based on decentralised government using direct democracy, and is a practical expression of a political philosophy I call Free Democracy - which is partly Libertarian, partly Anarchic; and whose economic principle is called EnMo (short for Enough and More), an economic philosophy that's partly Socialist and partly Capitalist. It attempts to extract the good ideas of these

9

models (good, that is, for Us, the 99%), and discard the less good. It ensures everyone has enough, but provides for those who want more to be able to obtain it. The People's Constitution tries to bridge the gulf between Them and Us by assimilating the 1% through the provision of universal justice that applies equally to 100% of the people - because until that happens the world will never have real justice or know permanent peace.

The People's Constitution confronts every recognised or established institution of power, and offers an alternative model. The recognised and established institutions of power are the true enemies of the 99% - because they exist to serve the 1%, not the 99%. They serve Them, not Us. Therefore they must be dismantled and replaced with something completely new.

If I had to identify just one important feature of the People's Constitution that's radically different to anything that's gone before it would be this: decision-making.

Almost every model of government that's existed for the last several thousand years has comprised some form of ruling body, and those who are ruled by it. Now, for the first time in history, we can communicate instantly with anyone anywhere. We no longer need elite groups of people making our decisions for us because of the excuse that information can only be supplied to those elite groups. That excuse no longer exists. Information can now be made available instantly to anyone, anywhere.

So the truly significant and radically different purpose of the People's Constitution is to describe a system of government administration that is, for the first time ever, wholly controlled by the people. It is founded on the principle that the people, *properly informed*, could and should manage their own societies. Some throw up their hands in horror and say what about the gangsters and psychopaths and murderers? How could you possibly have these people making decisions? **But what those critics don't realise is that the gangsters, psychopaths and murderers are already in charge - and always have been. They're the 1%.** We normal people are the 99%, and we demand the end of a system that allows our lives to be controlled by gangsters and psychopaths. The People's Constitution, because it is wholly controlled by the 99%, and a well-informed 99% at that, effectively removes decision-making power from the hands of the 1% – for the first time in recorded history – and places it firmly where it belongs: in the hands of the people.

Introduction to the People's Constitution

"Not only is another world possible, she is on her way. On a quiet day, I can hear her breathing." (1)

Arundhati Roy

Purpose: Although I regularly compete in British elections with the intention of completely reforming the British government according to the People's Constitution, at this moment in time this constitution is needed mostly for the reformation of the United States government. The People's Constitution should be a model for government everywhere in the world, and could, in theory at least, achieve that ultimate aim by gradually being adopted by smaller less-powerful countries such as Britain. But that would likely be a long and painful journey. At this moment in history the US is the global super-power, so it stands to reason that the best hope for a fairly swift and relatively painless introduction of the People's Constitution on a global scale is for it to be adopted in the US as soon as possible.

*   *   *

Take a human being, any human being: black or white; young or old; male or female; gay or straight; able-bodied or disabled; city dweller or Kalahari Bushman ... **ANY** human being, anywhere on the face of the Earth. Guarantee that person certain absolute rights that provide for their freedom, security and happiness; require them also to accept that in exchange for that guarantee they must recognise that others also have those same rights; and ask them to provide a modest proportion of their labour (if they are at all able to do so) in order to help provide and maintain those rights. If such a simple bargain could be struck everywhere on Earth, and fairly policed, global justice would appear, Permanent War would disappear, and people everywhere would be pretty happy. It *is* that simple.

Striking such a simple bargain need not be difficult: a guarantee of personal freedom and security in exchange for a modest amount of labour – how many ordinary people would oppose that? Such a model would not be hard to work; but it would be hard to achieve because it would be obstructed every step of the way by the very same people the 99% mistakenly trust to lead them – the 1%. The 1% will always oppose such a bargain for the very obvious reason that it is not in their interests to do so. The planet is, and always has been, managed by the 1% for the 1%. Any other management model is simply unacceptable to them. This fact has been identified many times before. Here, for example is Cambridge economist Robert Nield, quoting from WS Holdsworth's *"History of English Law"*:

> *"It followed that all those who, from their experience of the court, were most competent to reform it, were*

> *most interested in maintaining it in its existing condition."* (2)

And more recently ex-investment banker Nomi Prins:

> *"Unfortunately, the only players who have the power to overhaul the system are the ones who control that system, and they have too much to lose by changing it."* (3)

And even more recently sociologist David Whyte:

> *"A key World Bank document on "state capture" summarised this position: The capture economy is trapped in a vicious circle in which the policy and institutional reforms necessary to improve governance are undermined by collusion between powerful firms and state officials who reap substantial private gains from the continuation of weak governance."* (4)

So it's pretty obvious that the essential constitutional changes that we the 99% need are never going to be provided by the 1%. We will have to make our own changes.

The People's Constitution is not just another management model, which would be bad enough as far as the 1% are concerned, it's something much, much more, something much, much worse as far as the 1% are concerned, something the 1% will oppose to their last dying breath: it's a model that shows how we the 99% can manage our own affairs without them. It proves we do not need a 1% at all: **the 1% are completely irrelevant.** It's a model of government that's the polar opposite of the system of government we're stuck with, a system that has not only failed us, the 99%, it betrayed us.

Background

The British government is almost unique in the world for having no written constitution. A constitution is supposed to contain the rules by which rulers must abide. Paradoxically, our government requires almost every formally established group, body or organisation in the country produces a body of rules by which it functions - so therefore obviously recognises the importance of a constitution - yet perceives absolutely no need whatsoever for the largest and most important organisation of all, itself, to have one. Equally paradoxically, it also dispels the view of some anarchists who argue that society needs no rules. In this sense Britain is therefore an anarchist society, because it has no written constitution, but this has allowed a craven and dysfunctional government to preside over us for a thousand years.

It's very easy to see that the absence of a constitution means the absence of rules, and whilst the everyday lives of ordinary people are completely buried beneath rules, regulations and laws, the tiny handful of individuals responsible for maintaining and adding to that overwhelming burden are themselves completely unimpeded. The New York heiress Leona Helmsley, a member of the 1%, infamously said that taxes are for little people. She could have generalised this truth – widely recognised by the 1% - by saying that laws in general are for little people, not just the tax laws.

Intriguingly, although we have no written constitution, until very recently we had an entire government department somehow dedicated to the subject. It called itself the Department for Constitutional Affairs; but in one of those endless reorganisations that has guaranteed Whitehall's survival for so very long the DCA has now morphed with the Department for Justice. (In other words, it disappeared.) We also have numerous individuals who are styled as experts in constitutional law – a marvellous accomplishment given that no such law can be produced for visible inspection.

No doubt these good people would point to such historic documents as Magna Carta and the 1689 Bill of Rights and, rightly, remind us of the fundamental cornerstones they once provided for human rights, both here and in the rest of the world (clauses from Magna Carta appear almost unaltered in the American Constitution and in the United Nations Declaration of Human Rights).

However, the Magna Carta was never intended as a safeguard for ordinary people. Its clauses referred to "freemen", who were a fairly exclusive club in the thirteenth century – when most of Europe still routinely owned slaves.

The Domesday Book, written not much earlier than Magna Carta, *"determined that approximately one out of every ten citizens of Britain was a slave whose life was totally under the control of his or her owner."* (5)

And of the 63 clauses which comprised the original Magna Carta all but 4 have been excised from current British statute books.

The far more splendid Charter of the Forest, produced within a few years of Magna Carta, and largely intended to provide rights for common people, is never mentioned in polite society and is all but unknown except to a tiny band of specialist historians.

Whilst the Bill of Rights was also hugely important in that it legitimised the ascendancy of parliament over monarchy, it failed to legitimise the ascendancy of the people over parliament, and continued to recognise the right for an unelected individual with a hereditary claim to rule as the country's head of state – principles that are hardly consistent with democracy. It even provided for our entire country to just be gifted lock, stock and barrel to powerful foreign elites from time to time – such as when the monarchy was presented on a plate to the House of Orange, or the Hanoverians.

Purpose of The People's Constitution

The mere existence of a written constitution does not, of course, guarantee some form of superior government. Zimbabwe had one, for example, throughout the reign of

Robert Mugabe, but no one would say the country was therefore a beacon of democratic freedoms during those troubled years. Also it must be said that every other country in Europe has had written constitutions for at least a hundred years, but these documents haven't prevented the likes of France, Germany, Belgium and Italy from enjoying their fair share of colonial exploitation and plunder. And today's greatest threat to world peace, the mightiest empire that ever bestrode the planet, the self-appointed leader of the "free world", is run by a government supposedly controlled by a written constitution – hardly a ringing endorsement for the concept.

So why should we bother, why should the People's Constitution be any different to other, practically ineffective documents? In other words, what is its purpose? What is it for?

Over two hundred years ago Tom Paine wrote:

"A man, by his natural right has a right to judge in his own cause... But what availeth it him to judge, if he has not power to redress?" (6)

This is a vitally important point, which helps to explain why other constitutions are relatively ineffective.

Nothing better illustrates this than the landmark case *William B Richardson v United States of America*, which was finally decided in the Supreme Court on June 25th 1974, after almost seven years of legal wrangling. To put it in a nutshell,

Mr Richardson, an ordinary US citizen, questioned the fact that public spending on the CIA was (and remains) secret. Mr Richardson pointed out that it's a requirement of the US constitution that *all* public spending be publicly transparent. The Supreme Court rejected Mr Richardson's case because, to quote Chief Justice Burger, speaking for the majority, *"[the] respondent lacks standing."* (7) In other words, as a mere citizen, Mr Richardson was considered too unimportant to question possible constitutional malfeasance. He did not have the "power to redress" that Tom Paine spoke of.

Unless the citizen can easily and directly access and use her country's constitution to protect their interests, that constitution is all but useless, as Mr Richardson discovered. In other words, the citizen must always be able to use the law in her own defence, and or to hold her government to account whenever necessary. The citizen must never be excluded from using the judicial system herself to defend her interests against anyone she believes is a threat. It's the citizen's right to be able to hold her government to account, and it's the duty of the state to ensure the citizen can exercise their rights easily, freely and effectively.

It stands to reason that if you are in a position to not only make a law, but also enforce it, you are in a position of considerable power. This position of considerable power has always been the privilege and prerogative of elites; it has never been an easily enforceable right of the people. The

People's Constitution provides that right, to the people and, more importantly, it requires that every official of the state – the administrators of the law - recognises that administering the legal right of the people is their first duty, **and acts on that duty.** That's what makes the People's Constitution significantly different. It provides the citizen with the "power to redress".

Throughout the history of mankind political power has routinely rested in the hands of an infinite succession of tyrants and groups of tyrants. Political power has never been the property of the people for any length of time. Although there have been many attempts (some moderately successful) at replacing the inevitably corrupt administrations such tyrannical power creates, the evidence indicates that whenever the very rare benevolent dictator has emerged from the darkness their reforms are quickly eroded once they die, and there's a gradual slide backwards to some variation of corrupt dictatorship; so these infrequent idealistic revolutions that have appeared from time to time throughout history eventually revert back to more normal tyranny.

Most British people labour under the illusion they live in a democracy, and think this gives them ultimate control over their leaders, and therefore that they have some control over the law-makers and their enforcers. An even worse illusion that most people have is that their leaders act selflessly in the interests of the people. The people think these things because that's what their leaders and the institutions that support those leaders constantly and continually tell them. It's an illusion (at best) because the people who actually design the laws that control us (those in positions of considerable power) are entirely different from those we think are leading us. The vast majority of our laws originate from unaccountable civil servants, or, in corporation boardrooms (which these days is often the same thing), not elected politicians – and never the ordinary citizen.

The only way in which this situation can properly be corrected is not by removing from power some particular individual or group of basically corrupt individuals and replacing them with a new individual or group of basically corrupt individuals who wield exactly the same absolute powers as the previous lot, and behave in exactly the same corrupt and tyrannical manner, but by **creating an entirely new and different decision-making system** whereby no privileged elite possesses that much power. The only way the ordinary citizen may be confident that governments are making trustworthy decisions is if the ordinary citizen, *properly informed*, is the person making those decisions.

The 1% can never be trusted to act selflessly in the interests of the ordinary citizen. They will always act in their own interests. They always have and, unless our political decision-making system is changed, they always will. The only people who can be trusted to protect the interests of ordinary citizens are ordinary citizens, *properly informed*. It's really pretty obvious.

In the *real* democracy proposed in this book, government is entirely subordinate to the People's Constitution, which is itself subordinate to the people, and can only be altered through and by the people. **The People's Constitution replaces human leaders but is itself directly controlled by the ordinary citizen. It provides the set of tools by which we the people determine how we live with each other, and how our government serves us.** The constitution should be entirely in our control, the highest legal authority in the land, the law with which we can defend ourselves simply, freely and unaided if necessary against other individuals or organisations, or the abuses of the state. This constitution not only provides for the citizen to personally bring charges against those who abuse its terms, it also requires that the enforcers of the law, and any other public servant, serve it as their first duty, disregarding if necessary any instructions to the contrary they might receive from any other public servant. In other words, this constitution, properly empowered, should be the only protection the ordinary citizen ever needs. It gives that position of considerable power (to make **and enforce** the law) to the ordinary citizen, *properly informed*, for the first time ever.

Readers with some knowledge of constitutional law will recognise in the following pages a passing resemblance to the Swiss constitution. I make no apology for that. Switzerland is probably the most democratic major country on Earth; and despite its landlocked position and lack of natural resources it manages to be one of the richest and most successful nations in the world whilst maintaining sound social policies and high environmental standards. Switzerland is alone amongst its European neighbours in having managed to keep its people safe from war for two hundred years, even when completely surrounded by it, twice. It alone in Europe resists the suffocating stranglehold imposed by European bureaucrats. Whilst I accept that the fact that Swiss banks have long been safe havens for the super-rich might not be entirely unrelated to some of this success, it still follows that there are some lessons to be learnt from a country whose citizens have considerable direct control of their government.

So the mere existence of a constitution is a vital first step, an essential cornerstone for the citizen to assume control of his government. Of course it can only be as useful as the state's will to enforce it and the citizen's ability to access it, use it *and control it*. The importance of this point cannot be overstated.

General Structure

1.   The single most important thing to understand about the model I present here is that it's simply a work in progress. It doesn't pretend to offer Utopia, or some timeless work of

perfection that must never be altered; it is simply my best effort so far to propose a starting point, a system of government that *could* deliver **real** democracy straight away; a system that gives real social and economic justice and real political control to well-informed citizens; a system that no individual, or small group of individuals, could ever lawfully dominate, control or manipulate; a flexible system that only the people can alter as and when they choose.

2.   Preamble. The constitution opens with a fairly sizeable preamble. Although this feature is common in many statutes it's often overlooked. It should not be overlooked in the People's Constitution because it has a very important and specific purpose.

Many statutes have been written before which were actually quite well-intentioned. However, because it's almost impossible to write a law which covers every conceivable situation for when it should or should not be used, clever lawyers have built highly successful careers for themselves on manipulating laws to suit the purposes of those who can afford to pay them - the 1%. In other words well-intentioned laws are frequently rendered useless, or completely misused, because of the difficulty in writing them tightly enough to escape the wiles of unscrupulous lawyers. This has resulted in many egregious wrongs - such as providing corporations with the rights of human beings, without any of the responsibilities of human beings.

Although it's probably impossible to draft a law that always does what it was intended to do, and nothing more or nothing less, we can try to clarify things by writing good preambles, and making use of those preambles when interpreting each article of the law. In other words the preamble could and should be used as an integral component of each article, to help interpret its particular purpose.

In addition, the preamble could and should be used when individual articles are changed in any way, or repealed, or new ones added. Are the changes consistent with the preamble, and vice versa?

The 1% and their lackeys will always be bitterly opposed to the People's Constitution, because it removes from them the exceptional power they have always wielded. But those people, or those who wish to become those people, will never go away so the constitution will always need protection against popular complacency which would inevitably occur after a generation or two of peace and social justice. Once people are reasonably safe from the wickedness of the 1% they will feel the battle is won and they can let down their guard. That would be a mistake, for the 1%, or those who would be one percenters again, will **never** give up. The preamble tries to protect against popular complacency.

The preamble also tries to ensure that the constitution always remains the property of the people, that only the people, properly informed, can ever change it. And it tries to ensure that the ordinary citizen can always directly access the constitution, easily, quickly and freely, to hold her government to account; that no judge or magistrate or any other servant of the people could ever tell any citizen they "have no standing" to use their own constitution (recall *William B Richardson v United States Government*).

Therefore the preamble is a very important and integral part of the People's Constitution.

3. The constitution is constructed so that each section begins with a brief note about its purpose. This is important, and serves a similar purpose to the Preamble. Justice has frequently been denied to ordinary people by the simple expedient of ensuring that only the privileged classes have access to expensive lawyers to twist and manipulate the wording of the law – often perverting the reason the law was supposedly created. The constitution attempts to provide a simple but powerful shield that any citizen could use for their defence entirely unaided by expensive lawyers; and the stated purpose of each section is meant to show why that section exists, to help when necessary in interpreting the wording of the section. Quibbling over the wording should never be given a preferential weight to the common understanding (i.e. common to the citizens) of the *purpose* of the section – it is quite impossible to draft a law that caters for every possible contingency, and this fact has aided too many of history's villains, and victimised too many of history's

innocents. A clearly stated purpose before each section is intended to provide an auxiliary guide to the ordinary citizens of judicial panels in Magistrates' Courts who should be the final arbiters of all constitutional disputes.

4.   Section Two is about the individual rights of the citizen.

The clauses about rights are especially necessary. Human rights have never been a priority of British governments - except to use from time to time as a cynical political tool. British governments have generally opposed anything that might loosen their vice-like grip around the throats of ordinary people. Possibly the most liberal period of our history occurred in the 1970s. Ever since then British human rights have been in decline, and at the turn of the millennium were deteriorating so rapidly that the grim social wasteland of the nineteenth century was looking more and more familiar. The legal rights listed here are largely consistent with those of the UN Declaration of Human Rights, and should be a basic minimum for any nation that calls itself civilised.

5.   Section Three is short but I believe fundamentally important. Rights should never be separated from duty: no one should expect their individual rights to outweigh their responsibility to respect the rights of others, to care about other living things and our environment, and their duty to take responsibility for their own actions.

6.   Section Four is an attempt to explain exactly how the citizen might take up their rightful place at the heart of government decision-making. Real democracy will undoubtedly be a popular and successful means of government - providing citizens are properly informed (i.e. given truthful, balanced and humane information); and the system by which it's administered is simple to use, honest, quick, secure from fraudulent use, and free to use.

7.   Section Five is, if anything, more radical than section four. It describes an entirely different model of government administration to any that Britain has ever seen. There are unmistakable similarities with how the Swiss government is organised. It is basically a decentralised federal-type structure, where counties, directly controlled by their citizens, assume responsibility for almost all public services in their areas. It describes a republican model where the head of state is elected, and presides over a basically small administration whose main function is to support and coordinate when necessary the smooth running of county government. The central premise of the section regarding the public services, and all the personnel who are employed by the state, is that the state works for the citizen, and is *felt* by citizens to work for them, *not* vice versa. The two most radical features of this section are the militia and the judiciary.

Britain's armed forces are a considerable power, and have been for many centuries. However, the "defence" establishment is little different to any other government bureaucracy, or any big corporation. Whilst recognising that until an effective world police force is in place Britain should be able to defend its borders and airspace, the duty of self-defence should be shared by all citizens and not extended (as it always has been) to waging wars of plunder and aggression in other people's countries by a mighty military machine directly controlled by the 1% - people who either personally benefit from the subsequent plunder, or who are related to those who personally benefit from the plunder. The fact that Britain's armed forces are almost exclusively led by its upper class is no coincidence or validation of particular leadership skills that are only contained within the genes of elites.

Justice cannot be said to exist until it is freely accessible by the underprivileged and until the judicial process is exactly the same for all citizens irrespective of their social status or financial position. So the judicial system described here is an attempt to provide affordable justice for all, and suggests a low level model for how I believe most public bodies should operate – by replacing the existing hierarchical management systems with much smaller public services with management responsibility devolved entirely to the site where that particular public service is being delivered. In addition, the significant difference between the People's Constitution and any other is the ability of the ordinary citizen to personally bring charges of alleged abuse of this constitution against any other citizen, or organisation, or the state, simply by applying to a magistrates' court, which is obliged to take action accordingly.

8.   In Section Six I consider the economy.

The economy of a society is vitally important to its wellbeing. The economic model used in the People's Constitution is called EnMo Economics. Although this model has similarities to socialism, it is in many ways unique.

EnMo stands for Enough and More. The model distinguishes between the main economic responsibilities of the state – which is to ensure everyone has Enough; and the responsibility of the private sector – which (properly regulated by the state) is to cater for those who want More, providing they're also prepared to work more. EnMo Economics proposes that people (not commodities or bankers) are the *real* engine of the economy. It requires the state to ensure that not only are people guaranteed not to feel the worst effects of economic insecurity, but that they may also live happy and comfortable lives too.

Consistent with the fact that this version of the People's Constitution does not pretend to be perfect, that it just tries to improve on what we have, EnMo Economics too does not pretend to be perfect – it merely tries to improve on what we have. Given that both our system of government and its economic model have both failed the 99% in spectacular style, improved models are not difficult things to propose.

The core and backbone functions of the public sector (and the wider economy generally) is the work currently done by the lowest-paid staff. Therefore it's essential that the state ensures these essential people have enough to lead secure and comfortable lives in return for a modest amount of their labour (20 hours a week, say). Huge salaries for senior managers in the public services, which are currently the norm, are a completely unnecessary expense - as the work of these people is in no way more important than that of the humblest civil servant. High salaries in the public sector attract the wrong sort of person: public service is about helping people, not profiteering. So controlling the size of payments made to public servants would be one way of controlling the inflationary effects of government printing whatever money it needs. But there are other important measures which could also be taken, such as ensuring that people are taught something about economics so that the 1% cannot fool them again in the future with their trickery and outright lies.

Without doubt EnMo will be attacked by the capitalists, as the 1% definitely have the most to fear. They will screech about inflation, for example – a much misunderstood concept. But any criticism about possible inflationary effects of EnMo (which is not likely to be significant anyway) must also recognise and take into account how very badly the existing system has mismanaged the economy. Inflation in the existing model has been cynically

31

mismanaged for many decades. The vast global debt, currently estimated in terms of hundreds of trillions of dollars, is too huge to ever be repaid – it can only be written-off. This is inflation on a scale that cannot be imagined – and it's been created by the existing parasitic economic system, which may yet have catastrophic consequences (previous catastrophic levels of inflation have provoked global wars). Such disasters could not possibly happen through EnMo, and the other provisions of the People's Constitution. (But it must be said that until such time as there is a genuinely just and effective global legal system, together with a genuinely just and effective global economy, any society will be exposed to the possibility of powerful external forces attacking it – which is the long and sad history of mankind).

Full recognition must be made of the fact that the original source and bedrock of wealth is human labour, not rare commodities, plundering warlords, aristocrats or bankers; so a healthy economy is one which encourages and assists any person who is capable of working to do so; and a humane economy is one which provides the basic conditions for a secure and happy life for all in exchange for a modest amount of labour - whilst providing more in terms of material riches for those who want more and are prepared to work more in order to have it. A general desire for a free market economy must not come at the expense of enslaving people, eradicating small businesses, vandalising the environment or scrapping human and animal rights. In other words, providing the basic essentials for people to live comfortable lives, having compassion for other living creatures and preservation of our environment must be the primary aims of government's economic policy. Private enterprise could and should be permitted to provide lawful non-necessities, luxuries and anything else that isn't seriously harmful to people, animals or the environment; and apart from those considerations, which must always be acknowledged as the right of government to safeguard, the state should interfere as little as possible with the private sector.

How the supply of money is managed in most western nations is a little-understood subject. Put simply it has, like most things, been managed for the benefit of the 1% at the expense of the 99%. EnMo proposes a monetary system whereby the printing and supply of money, in most forms necessary for the provision of essentials, is wholly controlled by government. This means that it might be possible to eliminate many forms of tax collection (as government will be able to produce whatever debt-free money is needed in order to run public services). Although this version of the constitution includes some details on tax collections, it is quite possible that society will eventually be able to dispense with most forms of taxation altogether.

The idea that government could and should control money supply will attract shrieks of horror from many. These shrieks of horror will come from the throats of the 1%, and their lackeys, who will fight to the bitter end to keep full control of money supply in their own hands. It is self-evidently not in the interests of the 99% to allow the 1% to continue to fully control this powerful lever of the economy - as they have failed so spectacularly to protect the interests of the 99%. So providing for a government which is directly controlled by the 99% to also control money supply means that the people also have direct control of this crucial economic lever – which is exactly as it should be, since it's the labour of the people that provides public services and creates national wealth.

9.   Section Seven is about freedom of expression, a core value for any libertarian and real democrat. This is a vital component of the constitution whose importance must never be overlooked. Political decision-making is the duty of the citizen – *properly informed.* Therefore whilst any individual or organisation will have the right of free expression, that right will be tied to a duty to not misinform or mislead.

10.   Section Eight attempts to make provision to protect our environment, national heritage, agriculture and natural resources, and identifies the need for ensuring good transport and communication systems.

11.   In Section Nine I try to address the issue of social welfare. It is the duty of any responsible government to provide some ultimate protection for its vulnerable people. Few people are vulnerable all of the time, whilst very many

are vulnerable some of the time. The permanently vulnerable should be permanently protected.

In keeping with the economic principle that the state should provide Enough, I introduce a variation on the idea of communes. The traditional model of a commune is usually a type of socialist island surrounded by a capitalist ocean. But given that EnMo is a type of socialist ocean, communes would be the reverse of their normal kind, and provide the sites for the relatively small private sector to function.

12. Section ten provides for the temporary suspension of Free Democracy, the core philosophy upon which the People's Constitution is based. This can only be permitted in situations of such dire emergency that the communication systems upon which Free Democracy depends are seriously destroyed or compromised to such an extent they cannot be trusted.

13. An Ethical Guide appears in Addendum A. Whilst Free Democracy provides for any individual to practice any religion - providing such practice does not infringe the constitutional rights of others - Free Democracy does not promote or support any established religion. The Ethical Guide describes a standard set of values of human behaviour which are supported by Free Democracy, and many of which are also common to most religions. Its purpose is to propose how people should interact with each other, all living creatures in general, and the environment. The Ethical Guide is not of

itself enforceable in law, but suggests a set of behavioural ideals which, if voluntarily followed by everyone, would provide global justice, permanent world peace and long-term protection of our planet.

14. Free Democracy depends on a reliable mechanism for the citizen to vote. The world is slowly becoming aware of the fact that elections have been rigged for many years by the powerful and cynical forces of the 1%, and it's therefore obvious that a secure voting system is created and used to prevent that happening. Addendum B suggests one possible model. Whatever model is used, it is important that it's simple to operate, secure, free to use and genuinely trusted by the citizen voters.

15. The organisation of public services in a Free Democracy is considerably different from the existing monstrosity we must endure, which in truth resembles some manic creation by Kafka, Dali and Orwell combined – which is the only way such an inherently evil system can succeed. Addendum C shows two diagrams to illustrate the differences.

Notes:

1. *"War Talk"* by Arundhati Roy - p. 75
2. *"Public Corruption"* by Robert Nield - p. 110
3. *"Other People's Money"* by Nomi Prins - p. 287
4. *"How Corrupt is Britain?"* by David Whyte - p. 7
5. *"American Holocaust"* by David Stannard - p. 180
6. *"Rights of Man"* by Tom Paine - p. 119
7. *"Blank Check"* by Tim Weiner - p. 226

Proper Information

"The general will is always rightful, but the judgement which guides it is not always enlightened. It must be brought to see things as they are, and sometimes as they should be seen; it must be shown the good path which it is seeking, and secured against seduction by the desires of individuals; it must be given a sense of situation and season, so as to weigh immediate and tangible advantages against distant and hidden evils." (1)

Assuming the absence of malicious external interference (which is not a safe or sensible assumption at the moment), the next most important condition required for the smooth and efficient working of the People's Constitution is that people are always properly informed - especially by the state and by those sections of the media whose primary purpose is to communicate information the general public are likely to believe is true. Given that the People's Constitution provides a model of government that's wholly controlled by the ordinary citizen, by us, the 99%, it stands to reason that it's vitally important to ensure the information we're receiving in order to make our decisions and choices is as accurate and humane as it's possible to be.

I cover this subject in some detail in my book *"The School of Kindness"*, but it's such a key component of a properly working democracy that there can be no harm in reviewing some of the more important issues around it. The better-informed reader will know that what follows is accurate. Anyone who might doubt that should refer to *"The School of Kindness"* where I provide the detailed evidence.

Language

The very language used by the 1% and their lackeys in the educational system and the mainstream media cannot be trusted. Words we the 99% take to mean one thing very often mean something entirely different when used in the service of the 1%. George Orwell knew this when he wrote *"1984"* and invented Newspeak to describe it. Although Newspeak is obviously fictitious, the cynical corruption of language by the 1% that Newspeak describes is very real, and very dangerous. This situation is so serious that whenever we hear our leaders speaking it is always safer to assume they're either lying or deliberately misleading us, rather than to assume they're speaking the truth or guiding us. This is obviously an intolerable state of affairs.

Therefore the importance of the proper use of language is vital to obtaining proper information. This would not be difficult to do. But first there's a requirement to understand the very real existence of the problem of corrupt language, a situation that's intentionally and routinely maintained by the 1% and their lackeys.

Education

The problem begins when we are very young. Our education system fails the 99%, and always has. Historian Michael Parenti describes the problem like this:

> *"To say that schools fail to produce an informed, critically minded, democratic citizenry is to overlook the fact that schools were never intended for that purpose. Their mission is to turn out loyal subjects who do not challenge the existing corporate-dominated social order. That the school has pretty much fulfilled its system-sustaining role is no accident. The educational system is both a purveyor of the dominant political culture and a product of it."*
> (2)

But it not only fails the 99%, it fails the 1% too; but because the 1% benefit so hugely from this failure few of them would see it as a failure. But it does fail them too. It fails them because it brainwashes them to accept as normal an evil dystopian society that causes needless suffering and environmental vandalism that's permanently destroying the very means of our existence. The children of the 1% are brainwashed to believe "There Is No Alternative" to this, and that they are the chosen select few who must ensure that it's never changed. The children of the 1% are coerced to believe this nonsense by being taught to fear the 99%, to fear the 99% would put an end to their privileged pampered lives. In other words the children of the 1% are taught to perpetuate the evil over which they will preside and for which they will be responsible, and they're taught to ignore the global suffering and environmental catastrophes which they and their lackeys will continue to cause, because "There Is No Alternative".

The children of the 99% are similarly conditioned, that "There Is No Alternative", but they're conditioned to accept the automatic right of the 1% to rule them, conditioned to trust these people to look after and protect them. The children of the 99% are brainwashed to believe this nonsense by being told that they too could be one-percenters, and swap their lives of poverty and hardship for a life of luxury. All they have to do is work very, very hard. In the US it even has a name: the "American Dream". The lesson is taught by using the old carrot and stick principle. The children of the 1% are conditioned to fear the stick whilst the children of the 99% are conditioned to desire the carrot. The "American Dream" is actually a fine example of the cynicism of the system: it loudly promotes the stories of the tiny minority of people who do indeed achieve fame and fortune (but not always accurately), whilst ignoring the stories of the millions who do not.

The families of all these children are every bit as culpable for perpetuating this brainwashing as the education system itself - because they were also raised by the same system, and have bought into the "No Alternative" lie. They perpetuate it because they themselves don't know any different. Many don't even want to know any different, and are perfectly content in their conditioned state of permanent stupor, like battery chickens or lab rats.

In other words, a fundamental cornerstone of the misinformation with which 100% of us are fed every day of our lives - that "There Is No Alternative" - is learnt in childhood, through our families and in our schools and universities, relying on our conditioned unquestioning trust in those institutions.

There are always alternatives, and to believe "There Is No Alternative" to the evil dystopian system that rules our planet is not only demonstrably wrong, it's actually very stupid. *"School of Kindness"* provides plentiful evidence of this claim - and this book provides hard evidence of one possible alternative.

The Media

The philosopher Bertrand Russell is credited with saying that *"Man is born ignorant, not stupid; it's education that makes him stupid"*. To a very large extent that's perfectly true. Russell could have added *"And the mainstream media ensures he stays stupid"*. Once conditioned by the education system into our roles in life, of master or servant, the mainstream media take over.

The primary purpose of the mainstream media is to continually reinforce the brainwashing of childhood. There are two distinct components of the system - the so-called "news" media, and the world of "entertainment". Of the two, the so-called "news" media is by far the most cynical, because we believe the "news" is truthful and therefore trust it; whereas most people realise that non-news "entertainment" is seldom based on truth.

We're conditioned to believe that the daily "news" is true - especially when provided by well-established institutions such as the BBC or The Times newspaper. Although some of the details we hear on the "news" are indeed sometimes accurate, many are not. Some are outright lies. And vast amounts of truth are carefully ignored. This careful blend of truth and fiction, crafted by editors carefully selected to produce the correct end-product, is invariably easy to believe as it repeats the programming acquired in childhood - that our great trusted leaders, and their armies of "experts", although sometimes capable of "mistakes" and human weakness, can always be trusted to look after us and protect us. That our great trusted leaders always operate in the utmost secrecy is nothing for us to worry about, we should just go back to sleep and trust them to continue looking after us. It's obviously a very stupid thing to do; given the vast quantity of evidence proving that fact, but the vast majority of the 99% do it, every single day.

The "entertainment" media is simply a modern version of the circuses used by Roman emperors to keep the 99% distracted from what the 1% are up to behind their backs. It's an ancient trick, and it works very well.

Aldous Huxley wrote the following in the foreword to his famous novel *"Brave New World"*:

> *"A really efficient totalitarian state would be one in which the all-powerful executive of political bosses and their army of managers control a population of slaves who do not have to be coerced, because they love their servitude. To make them love it is the task assigned, in present day totalitarian states, to ministries of propaganda, newspaper editors and school teachers."* (3)

We live in a totalitarian state, a ruthless fascist world controlled by international banks and trans-national corporations who routinely operate in absolute secrecy. We think we are democracies, because this is how we're conditioned to think, at school and through the media. We think we are in control of politicians because every couple of years we're allowed to select one or two individuals from a carefully controlled range of options. We don't understand that our politicians are no more than glove-puppets, doing what they're told, not by we the 99% who elect them, but by the 1%, who pay their election costs and who occasionally admit them into their private and pampered world. The media is largely responsible for allowing this farce to continue, especially that section of the media we're conditioned to trust and believe the most, the so-called "news". It's the easiest thing in the world to prove the routine deceit of the so-called "news" media, it's there in black and white every single day of the week in every newsagent in the country, and it's there on our TV screens or radios every hour on the hour: so-called "news", which is seldom anything other than carefully crafted misinformation or distraction.

The great Australian journalist John Pilger describes how journalism *should* be practised, suggesting we should all be inspired by the American newsman T.D. Allman who, partly echoing Rousseau, said that,

> *"Genuinely objective journalism' is that which 'not only gets the facts right, **it gets the meaning of events right**. Objective journalism is compelling not only today. **It stands the test of time.** It is validated not only by "reliable sources" but by the unfolding of history. It is reporting that which not only seems right the day it is published. **It is journalism that ten, twenty, fifty years after the fact still holds up a true and intelligent mirror to events.**"* (My emphasis) (4)

The media, as it is today, is completely unsuitable for the proper working of the People's Constitution. It cannot be trusted to do what the 99% have a right to expect it to do:

simply to tell people the truth from a humane and compassionate perspective. Very considerable reform of the media is essential.

Conclusion

The purpose of this chapter has been to try to indicate some of the problems around the vitally important subject of Proper Information. It need not be as difficult as it is. Receiving good and proper information has always been made difficult because the 1% have always wanted complete control of information in the same way that they've always wanted to control everything else. That's why every government routinely cloaks itself in deep and often impenetrable layers of secrecy. We simply take it for granted that governments have a right to do this and should behave in this way, but a mere moment or two of rational thought makes it pretty obvious they should not. After all, if governments were truly operating in the best interests of the 99% what reason could they possibly have for withholding information from the 99%? After all, if our great trusted leaders are truly acting in our best interests why not tell us what they're doing so we can admire their selfless efforts and re-elect them at the first opportunity? But not only do they keep many of their activities highly secret, the information they do provide is invariably misinformation, distraction or outright lies. And when, very rarely, brave individual whistleblowers do reveal to us some of what's really going on, our great trusted leaders respond quickly and viciously - ask Julian Assange, for example, or Chelsea Manning, or Edward Snowden.

Providing Proper Information need not be difficult. First and foremost it depends on the will of governments to be completely open and transparent. This openness has always been non-existent. Therefore the easiest thing any government could do to help provide proper information is simply to scrap most of its secrecy laws – together with the vast departments whose only purpose is finding out the secrets of other governments whilst concealing their own. Apart from the personal details of citizens it's difficult for governments to justify the need to keep their records secret. After all, as they keep on telling us whenever they create some new law to spy on us, if you're doing nothing wrong there's no reason to object. Providing the citizen is not harming anyone it is absolutely no business of the government what she is doing; however, the business of government, which belongs to the people, is very much the business of the people. In other words the individual citizen has a right to privacy, governments do not. This is the first step towards providing proper information.

Next in order of priority is proper education. Young people need to learn how to work out for themselves what the truth is, and then how to use the truth to make good and humane decisions. Closely related to the issue of proper education is the proper use of language. Although it's in the nature of language that it's often confusing, and it will always be like that, the issue about language and Proper Information is around those who deliberately make it confusing with the deliberate intention of spreading deceit. The media have long played a very significant role in this function. Once again, a proper education would teach young people about the devious tricks of the corporate media world, which would make it extremely difficult for the media to continue doing it.

So, truly open government, combined with a proper education system, together with a news service based on the principles of T.D. Allman, will go a very long way to eliminating the current problems the ordinary citizen has of receiving Proper Information - which will be an essential prerequisite for the proper working of the People's Constitution. Our existing education system and those sections of the media that supply us with our so-called "news" are completely unfit for purpose, and both need to be reformed such that the citizen is able to receive good and reliable information and able to interpret it in a truthful and humane way, information *"that ten, twenty, fifty years after the fact still holds up a true and intelligent mirror to events".*

Notes:

1. *"The Social Contract"* by Jean Paul Rousseau - p. 43

2. *"History as Mystery"* by Michael Parenti - p. 22

3. *"Brave New World"* by Aldous Huxley - p. xlvii (Foreword by AH)

4. *"Hidden Agendas"* by John Pilger - p. 525

Welcome to the world of EnMo Economics

*"In the mercantile regulations the interest of our
manufacturers has been most peculiarly attended to; and the
interest, not so much of consumers, as that of some other
sets of producers, has been sacrificed to it."* (1)

Adam Smith

*"I see in the near future a crisis approaching that unnerves
me and causes me to tremble for the safety of my
country...corporations have been enthroned and an era of
corruption in high places will surely follow."* (2)

Abraham Lincoln

*"All for ourselves, and nothing for other people, seems, in
every age of the world, to have been the vile maxim of the
masters of mankind."* (3)

Adam Smith

*"Capitalism is the astounding belief that the most
wickedest of men will do the most wickedest of things
for the greatest good of everyone"* (4)

J.M. Keynes

Consistent with the principle with which I started this book - that you, dear reader, are already fairly well-enlightened and know the basic truths upon which this work is based, and therefore do not need me to prove every word I say - this chapter also assumes that you already know the fact that the world's economy is managed for the convenience and pleasure of the 1%, and the 1% alone, at the expense of the 99% and our planet's fragile environment; and that you do not need me to prove this. However, if, dear reader, your awareness has not yet developed to that stage I would encourage you to read *"School of Kindness"* where everything that appears in this section is more fully explained and validated.

The economies of countries are vitally important. The history of mankind is little more than one relentlessly long blood-soaked account of how "great" historical figures have murdered, raped and plundered their way to power by ruining the economies not only of other countries, but of their own as well. It is the history of capitalism, and of the 1%.

Economic and religious philosophies are like guns - completely harmless in the right hands, destructively evil in the wrong ones. The economic philosophy of capitalism is, in itself, harmless; but it found its way into the hands of psychopaths. Over the centuries the economic philosophy of socialism tried to put things right, several times and in several guises; but as it's intrinsically more honest and just than capitalism it was always easy prey to the ruthless monsters who controlled capitalism, which has degenerated into a philosophy which was once described by one of its leading lights (Andy Grove of Intel) as being about "shooting the wounded". (5)

Today the received wisdom is that socialism failed. The numbers didn't add up. It's a philosophy, we're encouraged to believe, which is simply unworkable. Capitalism is all there is. There is No Alternative. Like so many other things we're told by our trusted leaders, it's a lie. Socialism never failed, it was murdered, by the utterly ruthless practitioners of its rival. Whenever socialism has tried to provide some economic justice, from the English Diggers and Levellers, through the French Jacobins, through the Russian Bolsheviks, through Europe's brief emergence into the light following World War Two, to today's last struggling socialist outposts in Cuba and North Korea, the capitalists have always banded together to crush the very real threat to their murderous existence - to kill off the terrifying threat of a good example.

Although socialism is infinitely better than capitalism as far as we the 99% are concerned, it had its weaknesses, the main ones being the creation of largely useless bureaucracies, and the difficulties people had if they wanted to become wealthier than others. Socialism failed to recognise that individual wealth is not the main problem with capitalism;

the problem with capitalism is the firm link it provides between wealth and political power. Wealth, per se, should not be a problem. The problem is allowing wealthy people to have absolute control of political power. There's nothing wrong with having a society which has rich people in it - providing those people obtain their wealth humanely and through their own hard work, and they have no more individual political power than the poorest citizen in the land.

EnMo Economics is an original philosophy that tries to combine together the best elements of socialism and capitalism, whilst discarding the worst. It stands for Enough and More, symbolising the different roles of the state and the private sector, both of which have vital parts to play in a healthy economy. The state is responsible for ensuring that everyone has Enough, whilst the private sector is encouraged to provide for those who want More.

A full description of EnMo Economics is available in my book of that name, so there's no point in repeating myself here. However, it has to be explained that the economic sections of the People's Constitution are based on EnMo, together with any other related sections - such as Social Welfare.

Capitalism, as it's practised, has pretty much brought our planet to the brink of destruction. Therefore it's fairly obvious it has to go. Socialism would be a far better alternative, but like most things that model too can be improved. EnMo Economics proposes one such improvement.

Notes:

1. *"Wealth of Nations"* by Adam Smith p. 841

2. Abraham Lincoln in a letter to Col. William Elkins 21st November 1864

3. *"Wealth of Nations"* by Adam Smith p. 525

4. *"Extreme Money"* by Satyajit Das p. 128

5. *"The Best Democracy Money Can Buy"* – Greg Palast p. 146

A Question of Conscience

"All national institutions of churches, whether Jewish, Christian or Turkish, appear to me no other than human inventions set up to terrify and enslave mankind, and monopolize power and profit." (1)

Tom Paine

"The whole history of man is continuous proof of the maxim that to divest one's methods of ethical concepts means to sink into the depths of utter demoralization." (2)

Emma Goldman

"Freedom, morality, and the human dignity of the individual consists precisely in this: that he does not do good because he is forced to do so, but because he freely conceives it, wants it, and loves it." (3)

Michael Bakunin

It's important to include a few words on the ethical heart of the People's Constitution which, because it's written by an atheist, dispenses with the need for priests of any kind. This is not to say that religion should be banned – people must always be free to believe whatever they choose – just that there's no role for priests in the *political* life of a country.

That said, it's vitally important not to lose sight of the point that Emma Goldman makes, that ethics and morality are almost as important to a healthy society as food and drink. However, no one religion should be empowered to sit as arbiter and judge of what those values should be. All of the main religions are founded on quicksand - fantasy, hearsay, unprovable myths and outright lies, and all the mainstream religions have histories of inflicting incredible suffering on others. Therefore none of them has any right to dictate the morality of any modern society.

Like every other section of this book, this claim is also further explained and justified in *"School of Kindness"*. So assuming once again that you, dear reader, already agree there is no formal place for religion in the political constitution of a modern country, I shall not waste any time validating this point, but reiterate instead the vital need for ethical standards in the constitution. In other words there's a very big difference between religion and ethics. **We need ethics, we do not need religion.** So The People's Constitution comprises a section called The Ethical Guide. I believe this is vitally important.

There are three main assumptions underpinning the Ethical Guide. It isn't possible empirically to prove any of them, but it's equally impossible to disprove them too. Given that these assumptions are intrinsically harmless it follows that the Guide is also harmless (except to those very few who would intentionally harm others, as it would try to prevent them from doing so).

The first assumption is the ancient and widespread belief known as **the Golden Rule - that we should treat all others as we would have others treat us in the same circumstances.** This principle also extends to animal life and our planet's fragile environment and ecosystems, taking the view that human beings are not the most important species on Earth, deserving privileged treatment. So the Golden Rule has a wider interpretation in the Ethical Guide to take into consideration all living things.

The second assumption is that the vast majority of living things want to live happy lives.

The third assumption resonates with the view of Michael Bakunin, that maximum happiness is best achieved by helping others to be happy too.

The importance of the Ethical Guide to the People's Constitution cannot be exaggerated. It has a similar role to that of the Preamble at the start of the constitution, and to the role of the "Purpose" section at the start of each Article. Taken altogether they should all help with interpreting every clause, to help ensure that the constitution is not misused and misinterpreted in the way that so many previous laws and constitutions are - often in the most cynical and despicable ways. Like the Preamble and Purpose sections of the constitution, the Ethical Guide should not by itself be enforceable by law. It is just a guide, to help interpret the main, legally enforceable, clauses of the constitution; and to help all living things lead secure and happy lives.

If everyone freely chose to live by the values of the Ethical Guide there would be little need for any laws at all. So it's obviously an important and useful component of the People's Constitution.

Transition

This chapter imagines the first exciting days following the election to power of the first government that enacts the People's Constitution. Because the differences between our existing ancient and corrupt model of government and the new systems outlined by the Constitution are so vast it stands to reason that the required changes be as carefully managed as possible.

Initially the People's Constitution will have a few enemies, but they will be extremely powerful enemies. Our society has always been run by the 1% - a tiny handful of immensely rich and powerful people who have always ensured that society is carefully managed to serve their interests and their interests alone. I'll repeat some of the thought-provoking words I used earlier in the Introduction to this book.

Here's ex-investment banker Nomi Prins:

"Unfortunately, the only players who have the power to overhaul the system are the ones who control that system, and they have too much to lose by changing it."

And sociologist David Whyte:

"A key World Bank document on "state capture" summarised this position: The capture economy is

trapped in a vicious circle in which the policy and institutional reforms necessary to improve governance are undermined by collusion between powerful firms and state officials who reap substantial private gains from the continuation of weak governance."

All of these people, the 1%, will fight tooth and nail to keep things just the way they are. They say that their interests and those of the 99% are one and the same. Some of them probably even believe that. But they are obviously wrong, and the desperate condition of our planet is dazzling irrefutable proof of that fact.

Although these enemies of the Constitution will be relatively small in number (the Constitution could only come into being by being freely chosen by a majority of citizens), they are immensely strong and utterly ruthless. They have access to vast wealth, and close links to other powerful minorities both inside and outside the country who will also be bitterly opposed to the Constitution (such as some priests, for example) – in case it spreads to the global 99%. They also usually have close allies in the upper ranks of the police and army. Similar reactions by the 1% of the day occurred in the past, immediately after both the French and Russian revolutions, for example. So the very first days and months following the enactment of the People's Constitution will possibly be the most dangerous to its successful introduction. Therefore some form of temporary protection for the new constitution should be built into those early days, a period I'll call "Transition".

The single most important action to take to help ensure a fairly smooth transition is to educate and prepare the 99% for the inevitable reaction of the 1%.

At the time of writing, the country has not yet deteriorated to such an extent that the only way the People's Constitution could become reality is through violent revolution. At the moment it *could* be introduced peacefully using existing systems, and this is obviously the preferred option. Once enough supporters of the People's Constitution are elected to form a government that can lawfully enact it using the existing system, the Constitution should not be repealed or amended for a transition period of ten years. Because there is nothing in the Constitution that would cause physical harm to anyone there is no reason to be concerned about giving it a reasonable length of time to become established. The People's Constitution makes no claim to be a perfect model of government, and it is intended that eventually the people should be able to change it as and when they like; but its ideas about what constitutes good government are so very different to what people are used to that time will be needed to allow the effect of those ideas to be properly demonstrated. Normal people (i.e. the 99%) will need to learn through experience that there's nothing to fear in the Constitution, and that in fact it will provide the best form of government that society has ever known.

That said, there will be losers. The 1% will be losers. They will lose their political power immediately, and most will eventually lose much of their material wealth – which is mostly ill-gotten wealth and fully deserves to be lost.

Initially an inflexible period of transition might seem unreasonable. However, every general election already produces a similar result. Every general election imposes a set of dictators upon the country for at least four years, a set of rulers whose actions will remain completely outside the control of the electorate for the whole of that period. These rulers will immediately proceed to impose upon a largely unwilling nation endless laws without sparing a second thought for whether or not the people might actually want those laws, or benefit from them. Furthermore, our leaders have often conspired to form 'cross-party alliances' in order to impose laws that should not be changed for considerable periods of time by the possibility of new future governments. Such conspiracies often result in leading our nation into illegal wars, or scrapping the few civil liberties that were once so hard-won. So in one sense, proposing to allow a transition period for something that is very much in the interests of the 99%, is little different from what we have long been used to, mostly without realising it. In fact an openly-stated fixed transition period with a definite end date is far more considerate than what we're used to because it at least shows the people exactly what's proposed, and asks the people for their agreement to try something new and different, together with their consent for allowing a ten year transition condition.

This period of transition is very important, not only because the Constitution will have powerful enemies intent on destroying it – especially during its first years when it will be at its most vulnerable – but also because with the best will in the world some of the changes proposed could not take place overnight, and a little time should be built into the process in order for the inevitable teething problems to be reasonably resolved. Although it will be possible to introduce some very important sections of the Constitution with immediate effect, such as the all-important sections on rights and duties, and the effective invalidation of any law which contradicts the constitution; but other sections will take much longer to implement (such as some economic reforms, creation of communes and changes to how the public services are managed).

During transition the Constitution should not be introduced piecemeal, and it should not be amended, but adopted in whole, immediately, "warts and all", and a sincere national effort made to support it by setting out to implement the whole of the Constitution as soon as possible. There will be no immediate need to formally repeal existing laws – that can happen gradually over time. Some existing laws and the Constitution may operate in tandem. The Constitution simply outranks any other law or regulation, so if a situation arises where an existing law conflicts with the Constitution, the Constitution will automatically prevail and the old law or regulation might be effectively ignored until its official repeal.

Also necessarily different from the steady-state Constitution is the appointment of elected officials. The Constitution requires that in the steady-state elected officials (MPs etc) have certain minimum educational qualifications and have already served at least one term as county councillors. Obviously it will not be possible to meet these conditions when the Constitution is first enacted, and a "transition administration" will need to be established where the qualifying conditions are waived. This temporary relaxation should not extend beyond the ten year "settling in" period of transition − but the required training courses for future councillors should obviously be designed and started up immediately.

It is essential that a basic electronic voting system for the new decision-making model is in place within the first six months of transition. The traditional decision-making system should be suspended in the interim in order to encourage progress with the new one (although provision should be made to cope with emergency situations). It is more important that imperfect voting systems are temporarily endured if necessary rather than to permit delays waiting for supposedly foolproof systems – delays the Constitution's enemies would inevitably exploit to maximum effect. It must be expected that such a huge constitutional change will take time to get right, but this must not be allowed as an excuse to delay it happening at all. They should also be decentralised systems. Each county should create and evolve their own system, fully expecting to make mistakes and experience problems. Not only will this expedite the process it will provide a variety of different and innovative solutions which will lead to evolving the most successful methods, which others could later copy.

Intimately connected to electronic voting systems must be a reliable public information service. As the infrastructure for this already exists, all that's required is for a change in media policy. The Constitution requires that people are *properly informed.* Once again, individual counties should evolve their own information systems; but the basic essential components must include equally weighted *factual content,* for and against issues, as well as equally weighted *opinion* for and against issues; and the process must always take place in a spirit of compassionate humanity. As Rousseau correctly advised:

> *"The general will is always rightful, but the judgement which guides it is not always enlightened. It must be brought to see things as they are, and sometimes as*

they should be seen; it must be shown the good path which it is seeking, and secured against seduction by the desires of individuals; it must be given a sense of situation and season, so as to weigh immediate and tangible advantages against distant and hidden evils."
(1)

Although this would be a seismic shift away from the existing public information service (exemplified by the BBC, which has always been an agent of the 1%), the infrastructure itself is sound enough and merely needs to be administered by the right personnel. As this should be a relatively straightforward change to make there is no reason why a reasonably effective public information system should not be functional within the first six months of transition. Directly related to public information is, of course, public education.

The People's Constitution has been created for a very good reason: because the people have been deceived and lied to for many centuries in order that the plutocratic 1% may continue to ruthlessly plunder the 99% as they have always done. This message needs to be widely and thoroughly taught through a public information programme as soon as transition begins in order that the people completely understand *why* this constitution is so desperately needed. This is potentially a massive project. The system of lies and misinformation that are routinely and continuously peddled to the 99% as truth is so huge and widespread throughout society that it will take at least one generation of committed re-education programming for the effects to be sufficiently diluted that people will be able to start thinking for themselves in a humane and truly rational way.

Because the public sector would be the largest group to be significantly changed by the new constitution, it's necessary that certain protections are built-in for the most significant individuals who will be directly affected.

The single most relevant fact to grasp about changes to the public sector is that in most instances the most important individuals who work in public service are the lowest pay-grade staff and their junior team leaders. Senior managers (effectively the 1% of the public sector) could disappear overnight without any noticeable difference to the services provided. Therefore the new public sector needs to be re-built from this core of relatively lowly workers. These people need to be taught the People's Constitution, and understand that if they wish to continue working in public service an entirely new mindset will not only have to acquired, but loyally supported. That new mindset is that the public servant works for the citizen, through the Constitution – not for some other higher-ranking public servant; and that the Constitution is their immediate and primary source of leadership.

The new organisation for public services replaces the traditional centralised hierarchical management structure with a decentralised lateral administration model. In the new model a significant number of existing public service managers will become redundant, and those who do not become redundant will no longer be entitled to the excessive salaries they currently enjoy. However, instead of immediately imposing new and drastically reduced salary scales on remaining managers, their salaries should be gradually reduced over the transition period whilst they oversee the reorganisation of their departments, until the new scales become universal. Ideally no worker should be made redundant without first having the option of re-employment, albeit in a different role and/or different location. The new model of government will still require public servants, even more than now, so plentiful options for re-employment will exist, but many will have very different and hopefully more satisfying jobs working directly for the citizen.

The existing public sector operates a system where public servants work for other senior public servants, who are either members of the 1% or directly work for the 1%. Many public servants are driven only by fanciful dreams of becoming senior officers themselves. It stands to reason that many are disappointed, as only a very tiny number of the "right" people make it to the top. The new public sector will require people with a totally different mindset, people who will be perfectly satisfied to spend their entire careers in the service of their fellow citizen; for all public servants will need to recognise there are no senior officers to serve, let alone become, and no elitist plutocracy directing operations to its own ends.

Perhaps the most controversial reformation of the public services will be to the armed forces. The People's Constitution expressly forbids military involvement in foreign adventures – unless assisting in a properly constituted international force approved by the General Assembly of the United Nations. Therefore Britain no longer needs to maintain a permanently standing army, navy and air force. Given the many centuries of foreign adventures by British forces this will initially appear a heresy of the highest order. However, there are a number of very successful countries which cope extremely well without having permanent armies indulging themselves in the plunder of foreign lands (such as Switzerland and Costa Rica, for example), and without attracting any noticeable challenges to their national security. So there's no reason to assume that Britain has too much to fear by adopting a similar policy. However, the Constitution recognises that until such time as a truly just and effective international police force exists there will be a need for Britain to be able to defend its own borders. So the existing regular armed services are to be replaced with an expanded function of the existing territorial services, whereby every citizen may be trained either in the part-time armed services or in a new part-time civil defence force, both of which are to be organised similarly to other public services rather than the traditional hierarchical model.

It is also vitally important to consider the changes to big business (small businesses will not be much affected, apart from probably improving). Because big business is largely responsible for many of the problems that have led to the creation of the People's Constitution, it will come as no surprise to see that the Constitution will eliminate many of the wrongs created by big business - which will obviously impact on the operations of some of these organisations. However, there is nothing in the Constitution that calls for the immediate dismantling of big businesses; therefore they could and should continue to operate for as long as they are able – providing they do so within the constraints of this Constitution. It must be expected, however, to see many big businesses fall by the wayside. The truly useful, productive businesses could and should survive; but as many big business operations produce little to nothing of any use to the 99% (such as investment banks), and exist only to enrich the 1% by exploitation of the 99%, the passing of these particular parasites will not be mourned.

Given these vast changes to society that the People's Constitution will induce, changes that will really need at least a generation to properly bed-in, it's plain to see that a transition period of ten years, where no changes to the Constitution are made, is not too much to ask for. Once the ten year transition period has passed the People's Constitution should be able to stand on its own, and be treated like any other aspect of government and fully exposed to the people to amend as they see fit.

Implementation

Sooner or later the People's Constitution will need a group of people committed to its creation to drive it through parliament. It is inevitable that not all the people in the group will agree with everything that's in it. That doesn't matter. The only part of the Constitution that requires the unanimous support of the group is the core principle: that the ordinary citizen, _properly informed_, must be empowered as the political decision-maker of her county, her country, and eventually, her world. This version of the People's Constitution provides an example of the sort of system that could provide that, together with other important issues which could help to make the world a better, happier place. It's these other important issues which will create dissenting opinions and which the enemies of the project will try to exploit to maximum effect. However, there is nothing in this model of the Constitution that could not work if given a chance, or is harmful or dangerous. Therefore the dissenters should simply agree to disagree, but leave the Constitution alone. Once the people are truly in power, and have benefited from the ten years of proper education that Transition would provide, the people will be able to change any part of the Constitution they think needs changing. The single most important thing is to provide a system of government where *the people, __properly informed__, control all political decision-making.*

Notes:

1. *"The Social Contract"* – Jean-Jacques Rousseau – p. 43

The People's Constitution

*(A Proposed Model for the Proper Government of
Britain)*

Contents

Section 1 – Purpose and Preamble

Section 2 – The Citizen and Their Individual Rights

Section 3 – The Citizen and Their Individual Responsibilities

Section 4 – Democratic Process

Section 5 – The Organisation and Responsibilities of the State

Section 6 – The Economy

Section 7 – The Press, Media and the Arts

Section 8 - The Environment and Animal Welfare, National

Heritage, Agriculture, Transport, Essential Services,

Communications and Natural Resources

Section 9 – Social welfare

Section 10 - International Relations

Section 11 – States of Emergency

      Addendum A – Ethical Guide

      Addendum B – Possible Voting Mechanism

      Addendum C – Organisation of Public Services

Section 1.   Purpose

General Purpose

The true greatness of a nation is founded on principles of humanity; it is measured by the freedom, political authority and security of its citizens[1]; how it cares for its disadvantaged people; how it protects and conserves its natural resources and environment; and how well it is regarded by ordinary people in the wider international community.

Thus the purpose of this document is to provide details of the covenant between the State[2] of Britain[3] and its citizens in order to provide those values. The People's Constitution is the highest legal authority. No other law, rule or regulation may transcend, conflict or take priority or precedence over any part of it. Any law, rule or regulation that does conflict with any part of this constitution, either in purpose or practical effect, will be disregarded and repealed. No person may breach this constitution, or issue to a third party any order, request or instruction that conflicts with any clause. Therefore it is the first duty of every public servant to know the constitution and serve it as their first and supreme authority.

Specific Purpose

To provide a system of government whereby British citizens, **properly informed**[4], are in direct control of all political decision-making, including government spending; and to provide a shield for the citizen, all animal life and our environment that may be accessed easily and effectively in their defence against anyone who threatens them or the rights described below. No one person should have more decision-making authority than this constitution. This constitution, under the full and direct control of a well-informed citizenry, shall be the supreme sovereign leader of the country. All government officials, no matter their status or rank, will serve and protect this constitution as their first duty. Therefore all sections of this constitution should be interpreted with this specific purpose in mind. The Ethical Guide is intended to be used to help with interpretation whenever constitutional conflicts arise.

Preamble

This constitution was drafted as a direct consequence of and as response to thousands of years of elitist exploitation of people and the environment in order to produce wealth and political power for those few privileged elites. Financial wealth is something that is unique to human society, but which is wholly dependent on human labour and natural resources. Society has previously been arranged so that tiny elitist *minorities control vastly disproportionate amounts of labour and resources, often with brutal and devastating consequences, and invariably without any thought to the general happiness of people, the welfare of animals, or the long term well-being of our planet. Centuries of elitist control has ravaged the planet and caused unimaginable suffering and hardship to billions of people. Such irresponsible behaviour is unacceptable. It is therefore intended to remove such power and control from elites and to produce a system of government that is firmly and unequivocally in the direct control of a well-informed citizenry. This constitution ensures that no citizen has any more political decision-making authority than any other citizen, and for the interpretation of this constitution, all citizens are equal.*

The People's Constitution is the property of the people, and only British citizens may change it. Therefore it is vital that citizens know and understand their constitution, and that children are taught about it in school. Future generations should always be mindful of the powerful forces that will strive to remove that control from the hands of the people in order to restore plutocracy. Therefore the citizen must always be wary of any amendments to this constitution – especially those that might erode those all-important popular controls, restrict human or animal rights, or threaten long-term harm to the environment.

The economy is a vital part of any society, and the economic security, rights and duties of the people are every bit as important as their physical security, rights and duties. Many centuries of tyrannical rulers have managed economies such that they and their close allies become extraordinarily wealthy at the expense of the people who provide that wealth. History shows that many of these governments have gone so far as starving their own people to force their subservience and allegiance; and sent the nation's young to distant lands to kill or be killed - in order to enrich the leaders of such governments and their close allies. This is obviously wrong, and any economic model that allows the people to be so abused cannot be acceptable. So The People's Constitution proposes an economic model whereby all citizens may enjoy free, comfortable and happy lives in exchange for supplying a modest amount of their labour to some public service; and it also provides for those who seek more material wealth to have it – providing they work more, and do not obtain their excess wealth by abusing others, harming animals, or destroying the environment. However, it must also be added that although this economic model is perfectly viable, it is also dependent on being left alone by a very tiny minority of people who would wish to see it fail – and such people will always exist.

Section 2.   The Citizen and their Individual Rights

Purpose – To enshrine the rights of the citizen to enjoy a decent standard of life, and freedom of thought, movement and expression; to stipulate specific protections the state must provide; to stipulate the right of the citizen to take part, if and when they choose, in the decision-making processes of the state; and to protect the citizen from harm inflicted by others. It must be the duty of the state to allow and provide for its citizens to live their lives as freely as they choose within the constraints of this constitution.

The citizen is a human being who:

a.   if at least sixteen years of age has the right to vote (or not to vote) to elect political representatives as well as the right to deselect those representatives through the Recall procedure outlined below (Section 5); and to vote (or not to vote) in any decision-making debate between his/her elected representatives;

b.   subject to the conditions of Section 3 below, has the right to:

        i.   unrestricted freedom of thought, religion, expression and movement;

ii. free education in a state school up to the age of eighteen years and, depending on their ability to satisfy academic or technical entrance requirements, free education up to age twenty four in state universities or colleges of further education;

iii. free and prompt access to all State healthcare services:

iv. the full protection of the State from any threat against these constitutional rights by any person or organisation;

v. seek employment in any part of the country;

vi. a contract of employment clearly defining statutory employment rights;

vii. work until whatever age he/she chooses;

viii. retire from work, if they choose, at the age of 65;

ix. access any information held by any public organisation except for the personal details of other citizens;

x.   privacy in their home and family life, including privacy of all their home and family mail and communications;

xi.   live anywhere in the country;

xii.   leave and return to the country;

xiii.   compensation for State appropriation of their property, or for any loss or damage caused by the State to their property;

xiv.   full, proportional, and prompt compensation for personal injury sustained by any action intended to harm, or through any wilful negligence by a known third party;

xv.   join (or not join) any trade union, political party or other organisation;

c.   has the following legal rights:

i.   they shall not be detained without their next of kin, particular friend, or legal representative being informed immediately upon their detention as to why and where they are detained;

ii.   they shall not be detained against their will except by due legal process;

iii. they shall not be detained against their will for more than 24 hours without being formally charged with a criminal offence;

iv. they will be presumed innocent of any such charge until proven guilty;

v. they will have equal treatment before the law, including the right to:

    1. know full details of charges faced communicated to them in a language they understand;

    2. be fully informed of any evidence of those charges;

    3. have defence witnesses heard;

    4. have professional legal counsel to act on their behalf;

    5. be tried quickly (within 3 months of being charged with a crime) in an official court open to the public, presided over by a legal specialist before a jury or judicial panel of citizens;

    6. be tried for civil cases in the nearest court to their home;

    7. not be executed or unlawfully killed, nor punished inhumanely

or excessively by the State or its representatives.

vi. they may personally require a magistrate's court to hear any charge against another individual, organisation or the State, for any breach of this constitution, but shall meet the financial cost of doing so unless the court finds in their favour; such hearings to be convened within one month of the charge being made;

vii. they shall be permitted to partake as members of judicial panels, juries or commissions of enquiry without loss of income or other employment rights;

viii. they shall not be tried twice for the same charge unless new and compelling evidence against them is produced.

d. shall not be discriminated against;

e. shall not be extradited to another country without their voluntary consent, or taken by force out of the country.

Children and Non-Citizens

a. Children under the age of sixteen years shall have the same protections provided by these constitutional rights as any adult citizen.

b. Non citizens facing legal charges in Britain have the same rights to due legal process as British citizens. Foreign nationals found guilty of criminal offences will immediately be deported to their country of origin after serving any period of detention unless a judicial panel convened within one month prior to their release decides otherwise.

Section 3.   The Citizen and their Individual Responsibilities

Purpose – To provide a causal link between rights and duties; that the citizen should understand that any claim to protection by the terms of this constitution is conditional upon their adherence to certain responsibilities. The citizen is required to accept the consequences of choices they have freely made, without holding liable any person or organisation not party to those choices. This section is intended to assist when necessary the interpretation of Section 2: when conflicts inevitably arise between individuals, each claiming the actions of the other to be a breach of rights, the rights of the person who first suffered material damage, loss, or harm should take precedence over the rights of the person causing the damage, loss or harm.

a. The citizen has a duty to:

i. understand, respect and abide by the purposes and terms of this constitution;

ii. abide by the laws of the land (unless a law conflicts with this constitution - laws conflicting with the constitution cannot legally be enforced);

iii. respect the persons, property and constitutional rights and freedoms of others;

iv. take responsibility for their own actions.

b. The citizen, the State and all other lawful organisations of any kind have a duty to:

i. be honest in their functions, operations and all interactions with the general public and recognise that the freedoms granted by this constitution do not include the freedom to lie to, misinform, mislead, cheat, deceive or harm any citizen in any way;

ii. protect the natural environment, conserve natural resources and treat all living creatures with care and compassion.

Section 4.   The Democratic Process

Purpose – To provide a system of administration that facilitates the sovereign right of the citizen to be properly informed [4] about political issues, and for the citizen to make all political decisions whenever he or she chooses to be involved in the Democratic Process (see Addendum B for a possible voting mechanism); and to ensure that any individual involved with the administration of that process fully understands the importance of their responsibility for its proper administration, and the severe penalties for any deliberate abuse of that responsibility.

Preamble

The citizen is the sovereign political decision-maker of the state, and prime controller of public spending. All government decisions, whether by local councils or national government, such as the election or recall of representatives, policy decisions, authorisation of public spending projects, creation, amendment and repeal of legislation, will all be made according to due democratic process, as described in this section. No public law, rule or regulation, at any level of government, will be lawful unless it is made, amended or repealed through due democratic process.

a. The Resolution

The resolution is the question or issue to be decided by secret ballot of citizen voters.

b. The Debate

    i. Debates will be publicly notified at least seven days before they take place;

    ii. Such notifications will be easily and freely accessible by any citizen;

    iii. Debates will be freely accessible and open to the public and media;

    iv. Citizens are responsible for keeping themselves informed about local and national government debates;

    v. Time allotted to each debate should not ordinarily exceed two hours and must be evenly divided between opposing views, at least one of which must always reflect the considerations, values and concerns of this constitution;

    vi. The debatee will be directed by an independent chairman who will allow only relevant factual argument or opinion to be heard, clearly

differentiating between those two types
of allowable content;

vii. At the conclusion of the debate the
chairman will summarise the
discussion, giving equal time and
weight to the arguments presented in
the debate.

c. The Vote

i. Voting will take place not sooner than
twenty four hours after the end of a
debate, and not later than forty eight
hours afterwards;

ii. Any British citizen shall be able to vote
in any government debate affecting the
area where they live or work or have
tax-liable property rights;

iii. The citizen will not be compelled to
take part in the democratic process, but
may choose to do so whenever they
please;

iv. The citizen will not be compelled to
vote;

v. The citizen may only vote once per
resolution;

vi. Voting shall not be weighted in any
way. For any particular Resolution no

citizen's vote will count for more than one vote.

d. Simple Majority and Clear Majority Votes

    i. When a resolution must produce a positive outcome, such as the election of people, the result shall be decided by Simple Majority – i.e. anything over 50% of votes cast (on the very rare occasions when the vote might be exactly split, a tie-breaker will be provided such that the voting period is extended for a further twenty four hours and those who previously abstained from voting are strongly urged to cast a vote);

    ii. If a resolution is for proposed changes to the law it shall be decided by a Clear Majority – i.e. 55% or more of the votes cast.

e. Constitutional amendments

Resolutions for changes to this Constitution must be open to the whole electorate, and will need at least 55% of the whole electorate (not just the number of votes cast) to vote in favour of the change.

f. States of Emergency

Due democratic process may be temporarily suspended only in times of national emergency (see section 11).

g. Proper Information

Any information supplied to the citizen for the purpose of helping them to make good decisions must be Proper Information according to the letter and spirit of this constitution. Such information must be factually correct, accurately reflect any conflicting opinions, and be mindful of the citizen's rights and duties as well as the other concerns and protections covered by this constitution.

h. Constitutional Malfeasance

Any State employee (elected or unelected) who knowingly misuses, corrupts or falsifies any part of the democratic process; or any other person who, acting in a professional capacity, deliberately misinforms others about any public debate, may be charged with constitutional malfeasance and brought before a magistrate's court. If proven guilty, they shall be removed from their employment and forbidden from working in any similar role again. In addition, depending on the scale of their offence, they may be fined up to half the value of their material assets and imprisoned for up to five years.

Section 5. The Organisation and Responsibilities of the State

Purpose – To broadly define the main components of the State together with their lines of communication and main responsibilities. No part of the system should exist unless the citizen has shown she wants it by authorising the state to provide the necessary finance, or by freely volunteering her taxes to pay for it. Any citizen shall be able to inspect at any time the financial records and accounts of any government office. Every person employed by the state (elected or unelected) should thus be aware that their first duty is to serve the citizen, not state officials or private business interests, by ensuring the citizen's constitutional rights and duties are acted upon and enforced in law; and to ensure that any employee of the state fully understands the importance of their responsibility and the penalties for any wilful abuse of that responsibility.

Preamble

Britain's governmental administration evolved out of an ancient system of tyrannical monarchy followed by ruthless and self-serving financial institutions and corporate boardrooms motivated only by maximum profits for shareholders. The government was therefore a hierarchical model consisting of people who served leaders within their own organisations rather than the individual citizen. Government has never been organised and managed as an administration system to support the citizen and real democracy. This constitution ensures that any public servant recognises the sovereign authority of the constitution over and above any other public servant, individual or other organisation, and always works in loyalty to and in the service of this constitution.

Britain shall be a Democratic Federal Republic whose sovereign authority is its people, and whose decision-making authority lies entirely in the hands of its people, *PROPERLY INFORMED*.

The State consists of elected and unelected officials, none of whom is more important than or outranks any other. The State consists of County Councils, the Senate, the Presidency, Parliament, and the Administration. Individual counties will have direct responsibility for the administration of county government within the constraints of this constitution. Central government administration will serve to help coordinate the activities of counties, when requested by the counties to do so, and will represent the nation of Britain at home and abroad, but has no controlling authority over any individual council unless it fails to function according to this constitution.

Councillors, MPs, Senators and the President are all elected by the citizens, are directly accountable to their constituents, and may be dismissed from office by the citizens. All council and national elections and any other administration of the Democratic Process shall be fully financed by the State. Private finance of election campaigns will be regulated by statute such that no candidate in any particular election will be financially disadvantaged by his or her competitors. Private financial support for any particular position in any public debate will be regulated by statute such that no person or position will be favoured or disadvantaged for financial reasons.

No elected official outranks any other, as all administration decisions will be made democratically by those directly involved; no elected official has any decision-making authority over any other elected official; and all receive the same conditions of service as Administration Managers. Public sector salaries and conditions of service will be reviewed not sooner than three years following a general election, and any changes to those salaries and conditions of service must be approved by the electorate. All elected positions are for a maximum term of four years at the end of which time they must be vacated. However, previously elected officials may stand for re-election.

Recall.

Any elected official may be deselected from office if a Recall appeal by citizens so determines. Recall procedure shall be instigated if at least thirty four per cent of a statistically valid sample[5] of voters in the area represented by that official petition for their removal from office. The state will publish data stipulating what constitutes a statistically valid sample for any constituency and update the data (if necessary) on an annual basis. The petition shall include a written statement of the reason for the petition in not more than 250 words. The office must be resigned within five days of a lawful petition being delivered and new elections for that office immediately arranged. The Recalled representative may stand for re-election but must answer the Recall petition in a written statement of not more than 250 words. The newly elected (or re-elected) official shall serve out the remaining time for that office.

   a. Public Servants

      A public servant is any employee of the state, comprising both elected and unelected officials. Their first duty is to know this constitution and to serve the citizen through the proper administration of this constitution, disregarding (if necessary) any instruction they receive to the contrary. If any public servant ever needs to disregard any such instruction in order to serve this constitution they will not be subjected to any disciplinary action, but may refer the matter (if necessary) to a magistrate for a judicial panel decision.

b. Financial Control of Public Services.

All public services will be wholly and directly financed by county and/or State Treasuries, which offices will be responsible for authorising, monitoring and reporting all public expenditure. All public services will make public every year a precise account of how public money has been used. That account will relate to the previous complete financial year, and the records of each and every accounting unit will be complete and accurate to within £100.

c. The Electorate:

  i. is the sovereign decision-making authority of Britain. Only the electorate has the power to elect and recall local councillors, MPs, senators and the president; and the authority to initiate, make, change and repeal laws; and decide how public money is spent;

ii. comprises all British citizens sixteen years of age and older;

iii. is responsible for overseeing the administration of justice by partaking in juries, judicial panels and commissions of inquiry.

d. Any citizen:

i. may petition for changes to the law and the constitution by obtaining 10% support of a statistically valid sample of voters from the area(s) that would be affected by the proposed change (50% support required for petitions to amend this constitution);

ii. may vote (or not vote) to determine the order of business in local council and parliamentary debate;

iii. may vote (or not vote) in any public decision-making debate;

iv. is entitled to access any information held by any public servant (personal details of citizens excepted – as in Section 2.b.ix and x above).

e. Elections to positions in the state administration.

  i. Any person elected to any government position must sign a contract of allegiance to this constitution before they may take up office, and their first duty will be to protect and uphold this constitution and defend the constitutional rights of all citizens;

  ii. no elected official shall ordinarily have any more decision-making authority than any other citizen (temporary states of emergency [6] excepted);

  iii. elections for all public offices shall be fully financed and administered by the state;

  iv. financing of or direct involvement in election campaigns by non-citizens, foreign organisations or foreign companies shall be prohibited and, if shown to have occurred, shall result in the immediate deselection of that candidate and a charge of corruption considered for the candidate and the person or organisation providing the funding, as well as any State official who knowingly participated in that candidate's campaign;

v.   elections shall be administered such that all candidates have equal opportunities to promote their candidature;

vi.   where the number of candidates competing for a particular post is greater than five, preliminary rounds of elections shall be held to eliminate by half the number of candidates. This shall continue until five (or fewer) candidates are remaining, which number shall contest the final round;

vii.   the winner shall be decided by a simple majority vote;

viii.   systems of proportional representation may be used;

f. County Councils:

    i. County councils are regional authorities responsible for:

        1.   drafting all by-laws for their county;

2. the collection and distribution of regional taxes;

3. administration of regional militias and civil defence forces;

4. the day to day financing and provision of all public services within their region.

ii All administration of public services and all political decision-making will conform to this constitution. County Councils will not ordinarily be controlled by the national organs of state (i.e. parliament and the senate), except under a State of Emergency – see Section 11 below – and will have the authority and the resources to administer their areas according to the constitution, the law, and the wishes of their electors.

iii Each council shall convene in a venue conveniently located for the majority of citizens living in that region. It shall be open to the public, and ensure its business, financial management, and decision-making procedures are open and transparent and controlled by the citizens who reside there. Each council may operate according to its own constitution providing it does not conflict in substance from this constitution.

g. County Councillors:

Each county councillor shall represent not more than 10,000 citizens. County Councillors must:

i. be British citizens, and normally reside amongst the people they represent;

ii. be elected by a simple majority of eligible citizens;

iii. have passed examinations to at least matriculation level in political history, English language, economics and public accounting, and constitutional law;

iv. serve his or her electors by ensuring the proper administration of this constitution.

h. The Senate:

The Senate is responsible for overseeing the proper administration of this constitution across the whole nation. It comprises eight Secretaries of State – individuals elected to head the eight government departments which are: Treasury; Health; Education; Social Welfare; Foreign Affairs; Transport, Essential Services and Communications; Justice, Civil Defence and National Security; Environment, Arts and National Heritage. Senators have no more policy-making authority than any other citizen. They are responsible for coordinating the administration of their departments whenever Administration managers (see below) require it; and to agree with county councillors national standards and measurement criteria for public services which, once established, should not be changed for at least ten years. The Senate is responsible for ensuring the principle of truly open government is practised and will, except for the personal details of individuals, ensure all government information is easily accessible and freely available for inspection at any time by any British citizen.

Senators:

i.   must have served at least one term of office as an MP or County Councillor, but cannot stand for election to the senate whilst serving in either of those capacities;

ii.   be elected by a simple majority of eligible citizens;

iii.   must be chosen not sooner than six months after a new parliament has been convened and not later than twelve months afterwards.

Chairmanship of the senate will rotate every three months between senators. The function of the Chair is to coordinate the activities of the Senate and its departments, and oversee the proper management of the national budget.

i.   The President:
      The President:

i.   must have served at least one term of office as a senator, MP or County Councillor, but cannot stand for election to presidential office whilst serving in any of those capacities;

ii. is the nominal head of state with overall administrative responsibility for representing the nation's interests by ensuring national constitutional integrity;

iii. is elected by a simple majority of eligible citizens;

iv. must be chosen not sooner than twelve months after a new parliament has formed and not later than two years afterwards;

v.   convenes and dissolves the senate and parliament as well as assuming responsibility for constitutional integrity of both houses.

j. Parliament:

Parliament is responsible for overseeing due process for public debates regarding national issues and drafting subsequent legislation. Each Member of Parliament:

     i. represents one county, and is responsible for overseeing constitutional conformity within the council responsible for administration of public services in that county;

    ii. must have served at least one term as a County Councillor, but cannot stand for parliament whilst serving as a County Councillor;

   iii. must normally reside in the county they represent;

   iv. must be chosen by the electors of that county.

k. The Administration:

The Administration comprises the body of unelected public servants who are employees of the State. Public administrators will comprise specialists, clerical support staff and managers. (See Addendum C for possible organisation model)

     i. A specialist is any public servant who deals directly with the public, or whose primary role is in a professional non public-facing capacity such as accountants, statisticians and engineers, for example. Specialists are elected to their posts by the co-workers with whom they work. Although specialists shall co-ordinate their activities by consensus with colleagues, they are individually accountable to a manager;

ii. Clerical support staff are administrators appointed by managers and provide logistical and communications support for and between specialists and managers. Clerical support staff are answerable to managers;

iii. Each manager is responsible for the overall organisation of a specific public service, including budget management. They are appointed by and directly answerable to specific elected officials such as a County Councillor, MP or Senator;

iv. Public servants will have contracts of employment with a specific county, or with the state, offering similar basic terms and provisions to private sector equivalents. Pay grade structures will not exist. People doing similar work will have the same rate of pay and conditions of service irrespective of age, gender, length of service or location;

v. Decisions regarding all operational issues and how procedural changes should be made will be by consensus of those specialists and support staff doing the work;

vi. Lines of communication between individuals and groups will be between equals, not hierarchical structures; and administered by managers but not directed by them;

vii. Conflicts that cannot be resolved locally or through official grievance procedures may be settled in magistrates' courts;

viii. Any public servant (elected or unelected) may be individually accountable in law for infringing or failing to support the constitutional rights of citizens;

ix. The practice of a "revolving door" between the public sector and private sector will be tightly restricted, because of the vast corruption this practice produces. So public sector managerial positions may only be filled by people with at least five years unbroken and current employment in the public sector. Ex-managers from the public sector will be barred from working as a manager or consultant in the private sector in any field related to their public sector employment for a period of five years after leaving the public sector.

I. The Police

The police force will be the sole authority for maintaining homeland security. It will investigate all breaches of the law bringing suitable prosecutions before the appropriate court.

i. Each county is responsible for the maintenance and administration of its police force;

ii. Individual police officers will respect, enforce and defend the constitutional rights and duties of all citizens as their first duty, and may be personally liable for any failure to do so;

iii. Should any police officer receive an instruction that conflicts with any term of this constitution they are required to disregard it and report the matter to a magistrate's court for adjudication;

iv. No officer referring a constitutional matter for adjudication shall be disciplined for doing so;

v. No one shall be above the law, and anyone suspected of breaching national or international laws shall be properly investigated and, if appropriate, prosecuted.

m. The Militia

Except for a minimal number of administrators and specialists, Britain will not maintain a permanent army, navy or air force. The area of government tasked with the nation's defence will be known as The Militia.

Each county will be required to work with neighbouring counties and central government to train, equip and administer a militia capable of protecting British airspace, coastlines and mainland; and a civil defence force (CDF) capable of reacting to any national emergency.

On leaving full time education, each citizen will be required to serve for one year in either the militia or civil defence force, and attend annual one-week training camps until they are fifty years of age. Citizens may continue to attend training camps after age fifty if they choose to do so.

i. The first duty of the militia and CDF is to serve the sovereign people of Britain through this constitution, and should they receive an instruction that conflicts with any term of this constitution they are required to disregard it and report the matter to a magistrate's court for adjudication;

ii. No volunteer referring a constitutional matter for adjudication shall be disciplined for doing so;

iii. Militia officers will be answerable to the MP of the county where they are based who will be their nominal commanding officer;

iv. The militia will only serve in cooperation with British officers (unless if required to do so under para vi below), and those officers will only serve this constitution;

v. No member of the militia will bear arms against any unarmed citizen of Britain or the British Commonwealth; nor take or destroy the property of any citizen of Britain or the British Commonwealth;

vi. No member of the militia will take part in any war outside the territorial limits of Britain or the British Commonwealth, except as part of a properly constituted force legally authorised by the General Assembly of the United Nations;

vii. Workers in the militia or civil defence have the right to compensation from the state for loss of earnings, or for injuries sustained, whilst on duty.

viii. Militia workers will be taught about the Geneva Conventions, the United Nations Charter and Declaration of Human Rights and any other relevant international laws regarding wars and human rights; and each volunteer will be individually responsible for adhering to those laws – disregarding any instruction he or she might receive to the contrary. Anyone who refuses to obey an instruction that might contravene this constitution or international law will not be disciplined for doing so.

n. The Judiciary

Justice is administered according to the principle that justice is what the ordinary citizen, *properly informed*, says it is. Although the State will have legal specialists of different types, none of them will have more decision-making authority than citizens, *properly informed*, serving in their capacity as members of properly constituted tribunals or juries.

The Judiciary comprises those administrators specialised in ensuring that justice is provided. It includes judges, magistrates, public defenders and prosecutors, adjudicators and court officials. Judges preside in high courts and are specialists in criminal and company law whilst magistrates are specialists in constitutional, civil, contract and employment law.

High court verdicts will be decided by juries each comprising twelve citizens randomly selected from the local voters' roll. Magistrate's court verdicts will be decided by a panel of four citizens randomly selected from the local voters' roll, the magistrate voting only where the citizens' decisions are equally split.

    i.   The judiciary is financed directly by the Treasury, and is independent of any controls other than the law and this constitution;

   ii.   Judges are appointed by the state, and treated as public sector specialists. They must have an appropriate law degree as well as at least five years experience working in some other capacity within the judiciary;

iii. Whilst previous similar cases may be cited for purposes of legal argument, such cases will not establish binding precedent, and every hearing will be considered and decided solely on its own unique circumstances;

iv. Whilst the letter of the law must be considered in all cases, it will be secondary in consideration to the purpose for which a law was made, and arriving at a just and humane conclusion;

v. Citizens are required to take responsibility for their own actions, and no question of compensation from the state will be considered in situations where citizens have freely chosen to ignore obvious potential hazards or risks, or where intentional harm or careless negligence against them cannot be established.

Magistrates' Courts

The primary purpose of a Magistrate's Court is to resolve and punish when necessary any infringements of this constitution. It also resolves breaches of civil law, and may also be called upon to help resolve any conflict between disputing parties where no other formal mechanism for appropriate conflict resolution exists.

Any citizen may apply to a magistrate's court for a ruling on his or her constitutional or employment rights, or for help with any other conflict resolution, and the court is obliged to hear that application. The State authorities and individual public servants may similarly apply for decisions regarding constitutional or civil law, and those applications will also be similarly heard.

    vi. Anyone appearing before a magistrates' court will be presumed innocent of causing an infringement or offence until otherwise proven;

    vii. Citizens applying to magistrates' courts for a constitutional or employment rights hearing may incur costs for doing so, in order to restrict frivolous cases which bring the constitution into disrepute. The court administrator will decide if the court will charge for any hearing based only on the applicant's chances of success. If it is ruled that an applicant must pay their own expenses but their action is subsequently successful, the court will refund the applicant's costs;

viii. No citizen applying to the court on a question of their constitutional or employment rights will, on the grounds of cost alone, be denied the services of a legal specialist to represent them;

ix. No citizen applying to the court will be obliged to pay any legal costs other than their own;

x. No citizen applying to the court on a question of their constitutional or employment rights may be charged a total fee greater than ten times the local minimum wage hourly rate;

xi. Verdicts will be decided by a judicial panel comprising a magistrate and four citizens, the magistrate voting only if the citizens' decisions are equally divided;

xii. The court will have the power to reclaim its costs and award damages for aggrieved persons proportional to any injury or loss sustained, and will have the authority to immediately enforce its judgements;

xiii. A panel deciding a constitutional question may order any individual to produce specific information they may hold;

xiv. All cases shall normally be heard no sooner than one month and no later than three months after the initial application is made, and within four months at the latest. In the event of the four month limit being exceeded through suspected prevarication by one of the parties the decision will be awarded against the prevaricating party;

xv. Appeals may be heard at another magistrate's court, but at the appellant's expense. An appeal must be heard within three months of the decision being appealed. No more than two appeals for the same case shall be heard.

xvi. Retrials may be heard at any time after a court ruling, providing new evidence is found suggesting a previous miscarriage of justice may have occurred.

High Courts

All criminal charges and other cases not provided for by the magistrates' court will be heard in a high court presided over by a judge and jury comprising twelve citizens.

xvii. Anyone appearing before a high court will be presumed innocent until proven guilty;

xviii. If a jury remains evenly split twenty four hours after its first vote, the verdict will be for acquittal;

xix. The court will have the power to reclaim its costs from wrongdoers and award damages for aggrieved persons proportional to any injury or loss sustained, and will have the authority to immediately enforce its judgements;

xx. All cases shall normally be heard no sooner than one month and no later than six months after a charge has been filed. In the event of the time limit being exceeded through suspected prevarication by one of the parties the trial will proceed regardless;

xxi. Appeals may be heard at another high court, but at the appellant's expense. No more than two appeals for the same case shall be heard.

o. National Statistics Office (NSO)

The NSO will be tasked with deciding and maintaining a Constant Measurement Standard (CMS) for all public services and the economy. This will be a set of statistics whose definitions and standards of measurement will be constant. These statistics must be directly relevant to the daily lives of citizens, and whose definition and measurement is constantly maintained until citizens vote to change them.

Other measurement devices may be used for specific temporary purposes, but shall not replace any part of the CMS system, unless citizens so decide.

p. The State Banking System

The state will maintain a public banking system, known as The People's Bank, which shall be fully independent of any private bank.

The People's Bank will:

i. be centrally controlled by the Bank of England acting on behalf of the Treasury;

ii. be locally controlled by a county council, in compliance with the Bank of England. The Bank of England will not interfere unduly with the relationship between a council and its local People's Bank unless illegal activities are suspected, or it is believed this constitution might be contravened in which case either party might refer the issue to a magistrate's court for a decision.

iii. be staffed by public servants;

iv. provide banking services to the county council, including money supply;

v. provide an option for limited essential banking services to those citizens who might want to use it (i.e. such services as current accounts, savings accounts, home mortgage accounts, and small loans whose maximum value shall be set each year by the Bank of England).

q. Corruption

Corruption is the misuse of position for personal gain or advantage. Any person acting in a public or private capacity who knowingly misuses their position for personal gain or advantage, or for the personal gain or advantage of someone else, may be charged with corruption and brought before a magistrate's court; or if they contrive to ignore information that results in such misuse they may be similarly charged. If proven guilty, they shall be removed from their employment, forbidden from working in any similar role again and forfeit the gain or advantage they made; in addition, depending on the severity of the crime, they may be fined up to half the value of their remaining material assets and imprisoned for up to ten years.

Section 6 – *The Economy*

Purpose – To provide economic security for all citizens, especially the least fortunate, whilst also encouraging small and medium-sized private businesses to flourish. To ensure the economy is managed independently of control by national and international financial institutions and is maintained under the direct control of the citizen; to find an equal balance between the private sector's right to make a profit and the state's duty to protect the citizen, natural resources, the environment and all living creatures; to define the boundaries between public and private sector responsibilities for managing the economy; to guarantee the right of the private sector to maximise profits within the constraints of this constitution, the law of the land, compassion for animal life, and respect for the environment and human rights.

The marketplace shall be regulated to ensure that:

     i.   *employee rights are protected*
     ii.   *consumer rights are protected*
     iii.   *animals are treated with care and compassion*
     iv.   *the citizen and the state shall both be entitled to own land and property*
     v.   *consumer choice is delivered*
     vi.   *small business is nurtured*
     vii.   *rogue trading is prevented*

viii. banks and financial services are entirely fit for purpose

ix. basic insurance services are affordable for all workers, and are entirely fit for purpose

Counties shall be economically autonomous, taking full responsibility for managing their own economies within the constraints of the constitution.

Taxation will normally be waived for low income earners, and will not otherwise normally exceed 10% of income (but the top 5% of individual earners and businesses may be taxed up to 25%). Capital flow into and from the country will be managed in such a way that all individuals, businesses and institutions honour their financial obligations to each other, and to the state.

Public spending shall be transparent with all financial records freely available to the public. Public service departments will be directly funded from county and/or state treasuries, such funding to be administered by public banks. State investment in counties shall be in inverse proportion to the per capita income in those counties.

Core Monetary Principles:

a. This section assumes the use of a monetary system based on EnMo Economics which proposes that the state is wholly responsible for the production and supply of money used by the public sector, and that a system of demurrage is used to help control money inflation in the public sector.

b. To recognise and value the fact that the work of the individual citizen is the foundation of all wealth; and therefore that the work of a citizen should have a marketable monetary value such that a good standard of living, together with all the entitlements and protections of this constitution, may be provided in exchange for a maximum of twenty hours of work per week for the State; and that the citizen may, if they choose and only if they choose, work for more than twenty hours a week and personally profit from that extra work if they so wish.

c. The creation and supply of money used for any commercial purpose shall be controlled and regulated by central government, and managed such that:

> *i. the State will not incur debts to foreign or domestic private banks for the purposes of providing essential infrastructure and funding public services, but will use public banks instead to create whatever money it needs for these purposes - such money to be properly accounted for and audited by Bank of England and or Treasury officials, such*

accounts to be always available for public inspection;

ii. any foreign national debts incurred by the State must be repayable in full within 12 months of incurring them;

iii. other economic principles of this constitution are fully complied with.

Preamble

Throughout most of Britain's recorded history its economy has been controlled and managed by tiny groups of immensely powerful people. With very few exceptions these people managed the economy for their own narrow purposes and self-interest. The interests of the vast majority of Britain's people, let alone its animals, wildlife and natural environment, have almost always been irrelevant to these elitist rulers except when they could be used as a means of increasing their already vast personal riches. These economic policies have resulted in causing many centuries of considerable suffering and injustice and environmental destruction, both in Britain and around the world. They are obviously abhorrent economic practices. This Constitution in general and this Section in particular strive to reverse these long-standing and well-established wrongs and injustices, and create an economy that removes control from the hands of tiny groups of all-powerful people, democratising it so it is entirely self-sufficient for essential goods and services, sustainable in the long term, harmless to the environment and provides real economic justice for all Britain's people.

a. Ownership of Land

Purpose

All land shall be vested in the State, which shall have a duty of care to ensure it is properly used to benefit the nation as a whole, with a particular responsibility to preserve natural resources, protect national parks and wildlife and maintain a secure, healthy and happy living environment for all citizens.

The State may invest its land holdings in a public bank, and the profits of such holdings shall be reinvested in the maintenance of State land, or the provision of public services.

i. The State will:

1. ensure that sufficient land is preserved for farming, market gardens and allotments such that the country is always able to provide enough vegan food for its own consumption;

2. ensure that undeveloped land such as national parks, woodland, forests, moors and wetlands remain undeveloped (except where development is required for their protection or preservation);

3.   prohibit waterways, natural lakes and coastlines from being privately owned;

4. ensure that undeveloped land, waterways, natural lakes and coastlines are free to roam, though such rights might be confined to footpaths where it can be shown that such a restriction is necessary for preservation of the land or protection of wildlife, livestock and natural flora;

5. ensure that a citizen is able to own land and property to develop and use for their home or place of business, providing that land or property comprises either their main place of residence or their main place of business. However, that citizen shall not have an automatic right of ownership of any fauna or flora living on the land, nor any automatic right of ownership to natural resources above or below the ground. Any citizen who wilfully and carelessly ignores this duty of care to the land and its fauna and flora may forfeit to the State their material possessions, and or be

imprisoned, and or lose any future right to ownership of land.

6. ensure that all public highways and other public rights of way are free for anyone to use and are maintained in a sound and safe condition;

7. own at least one large public park in every community where any citizen may freely meet and assemble with other citizens – providing always that such assemblies do not prevent the rights of other citizens, or harm the land, environment or animal life;

8. provide for land to be used for temporary industrial development, but shall ensure that an amount of money is provided for the cost of returning the land to such a condition where it may be used for agriculture, allotments, public recreation or for some other public purpose once its industrial purpose is no longer required; such an amount of money to be made available before any development takes place, and securely invested such that

it cannot be devalued or used for any purpose other than returning the land to public use;

9. manage the mining and use of rare or irreplaceable resources such that the State as a whole shall benefit;

10. ensure that land is provided for street markets to operate and small businesses to be nurtured, such land to be made available at a nominal cost to the market trader/ small business person;

11. own sufficient land for the purpose of ensuring that no one is homeless unless they choose to be, and will ensure that any public housing is safe, secure and entirely fit for purpose.

ii. A citizen shall have the right to buy or sell the land and property that comprises their main place of residence or business.

iii. Trade in land ownership shall be regulated by statute such that profiteering is prevented, and managed in such a way that local residents have the right of first refusal to buy land at prices they can reasonably afford.

iv. The activities of landlords shall be regulated by statute such that profiteering from rented property is forbidden and that rented property is safe, secure and fit for purpose. Tenancy agreements shall be required to meet statutory requirements with regard to providing safe, secure and decent accommodation.

v. Land used for public communications, such as roads, rail and waterways; or for essential services, such as supplying water, electricity, gas or telecommunications, shall be owned by the State (except where such services terminate at or pass through private property – but where the State may have right of maintenance access) but used in such a way as to minimise damage to the environment, not to disrupt farming, and constructed in such a way as to minimise public nuisance.

vi. Ownership of land by people or organisations living or based outside the country shall not be permitted.

vii. The State may (or may not, as it sees fit) own the land where public buildings are situated, or where any State function takes place.

viii. The State may compulsorily purchase land providing it can be shown that such a purchase is necessary to the people living near to that land or if it is in some other way beneficial to the country as a whole. Where the State does make such a compulsory purchase it will pay 10% more than the commercial valuation of that land, by way of compensation to the previous landowner.

ix. The State may provide for community-based organisations such as churches, charities, sports and social clubs to use State land free of charge providing the land and any buildings upon it are maintained in a good and safe condition, are used for the benefit of the community as a whole, and are democratically administered and managed such that no individual or group of individuals profit financially.

b. Banking
i. The Bank of England shall be managed by the Treasury, acting on behalf of the citizen. Its management meetings will therefore be open to the

public and the media, and its executive decisions open for public debate and vote like any other government decision-making process.

The Bank of England shall control the issue, supply and circulation of the national currency (credit, banknotes and coins), manage foreign exchange and capital flows into and out of the country, manage base interest rates for borrowing and stability of pricing, set measurement standards and targets for monetary inflation, and assume responsibility for the proper policing of all banking activities throughout the country.

The Bank of England shall maintain stocks of foreign and reserve currencies and other recognised instruments of money such as gold and silver bullion for the purposes of facilitating international trade.

ii. Each county may set up and manage its own public bank, whose operating charter will not conflict in substance with this constitution. Such banks will comply with operating standards established and maintained by the Bank of England. County banks may print and circulate their own money if they choose to do so, and under the supervision of the Bank of England (such money to be used in addition to the national currency - not in place of it). Employees of public banks will be public servants, and profits will be expended on the county's public services and facilities, or to assist small business projects.

iii. Public (State owned) banks may be established wherever needed and will be overseen by the Bank of England. Public banks may provide citizens with savings and deposit accounts and offer any other banking service approved by the Bank of England. Public banks may create, supply and circulate money to government offices - such money to be used only for public services approved by local communities, and developing new community projects or works. Public banks may produce a unique scrip to be used to finance public services - such scrip to be recognised as legal tender. The administration of public banks shall be open to public scrutiny at all times, and they shall be regulated and audited annually by the Bank of England.

iv. Private banks may be established but their actions will be regulated, controlled and inspected by the Bank of England. At least 25% of the asset reserves of a private bank must be held in the form of gold and/or silver metal, and/or land, and/or a globally accepted fiat currency.

v. Clearing banks will be separate business entities from investment banks.

vi. The State will not serve as lender of last resort to any private bank.

c. The London Stock Exchange
The London Stock Exchange will serve as the market place for the trading of commodities, company shares and other business products. It shall be managed independently of the Treasury but shall have Treasury representation on its board of directors, and its business will be regularly monitored by Treasury inspectors. Its functions will be regulated such that its actions cannot adversely affect or influence the economy.

d. Insurance and other Financial Services
Insurance and other financial services shall be regulated by statute such that their operations are transparent and fit for purpose.

e. General Economic Principles
i. The State will maintain a model of the economy that will ensure that every citizen is provided with enough to enjoy a secure and happy life in return for which every working-age citizen will be expected to work for up to 20 hours per week in some public service (if able to do so).

The State will also provide for the private sector to supply lawful non-essential products or services at whatever profits it can achieve.

When asked by the citizen to do so, the State has a duty to provide the citizen with certain essential goods, utilities and services free and without charge in accordance with its responsibilities under this constitution, or at reasonable prices - depending on the economic circumstances of the citizen. The prices of such essential goods, utilities and services will be set by the Public Bank in the area where the transaction takes place, and the quality and minimum quantity per person are to be defined by statute, and may not be sold or traded by the recipient citizen to any third party. Any other goods, utilities and services that are not deemed essential by statute, and are not specifically proscribed by law, may be provided and traded by the private sector, at whatever profit margin they see fit.

ii. Central government shall aim to achieve balanced economic development throughout the country, especially with regard to eliminating involuntary unemployment, and controlling capital flight, inflation and base interest rates. The State will support and nurture the business community, but the business community must recognise and accept their social responsibilities to employees and citizens, and their duty to protect the environment, animal welfare and natural resources, as described in this constitution. The State will encourage long term sustainable business strategies; and though it may allow private individuals or companies to undertake high risk business ventures, the State will not finance or underwrite those ventures or relieve them if they fail.

iii. Although the general principle of economic freedom will be applied throughout the country, central and local authorities may propose temporary measures that depart from this principle providing such action is in the general economic interest of the people living and working in the areas concerned, and does not harm the environment, animal life or the national heritage.

iv. Key social economic indicators (such as life expectancy, average hours worked per week, retirement age, and unemployment) shall be clearly defined in terms relevant and significant to the citizen, such definitions to be constantly and consistently applied until the citizen calls for their change.

v. The government may propose measures when necessary to protect the domestic economy from aggressive foreign markets by:

1. reducing overhead expenses of small businesses through concessions on tax, rent and service charges;

2. providing vocational skills training;

3. actively encouraging development of environmentally sound and ethically manufactured products by requiring producers to provide accessible and accurate information concerning the origin, quality, production methods and processing procedures for their foodstuffs or other products;

4. managing import and export tariffs;

5. taking any other measure to promote the interests of the domestic economy.

f.   Machines of War, Weapons of War and Other War Materials

Britain will not permit the sale of machines of war, weapons of war or other war materials to other countries. Small arms sales will be restricted to state security services and those whose lawful professions or legitimate pastimes require the use of specific types of small calibre, non-automatic firearms (such as farmers, gamekeepers and gun clubs).

g. Animal Welfare

All businesses that use or deal in any way with live animals will ensure the very highest standards of animal welfare. They will not cause an animal to suffer pain or unnecessary stress; and any part of their business operation involving where animals live or work, or how they are transported, will be freely open to state or public inspection at any time. Penalties for animal abuse could require the closure of that business and the forfeiture to the State of the assets of the owner and managers of the business, as well as significant prison sentences for the owner, managers and all other individuals complicit in the abuse.

h. The Business Community

The business community will be independent of government controls with the following exceptions. It will:

> i. abide by this constitution and other laws of the land;
>
> ii. honour agreements and contracts which have been freely entered into, accepting the authority of magistrates' courts to adjudicate in disputes and to directly and promptly

sequester funds for reparations when necessary;

iii. provide all employees with contracts of employment defining their conditions of service, duties and responsibilities; and accept the authority of magistrates' courts to rule in employment disputes and to directly and promptly sequester funds for reparations when necessary;

iv. make available to State inspectors for their examination any property or premises owned by or related to the business, or any information about the business, within twenty four hours of being notified of such an inspection;

v. accept as payment for goods any scrip produced by a public bank at a value to be stipulated by the Bank of England, such scrip to be redeemable for that value at any public bank.

i. The State

The State:

    i. may launch initiatives to boost the economy in depressed areas giving preference to initiatives likely to produce or help facilitate long term employment and self-sustaining enterprises;

    ii. may intervene to protect the economy in times of national emergency, and uphold the law, or to protect small businesses from unfair competition;

    iii. will protect the consumer and business community by:

    1. providing an economic climate that supports fair competition between domestic suppliers of goods and services,

    2. administering national trading standards,

    3. preventing profiteering by suppliers of essential foods, medicines, fuel and utilities such as gas, electricity, water and telecommunications; and especially ensuring that these

essential items are available to vulnerable groups;

iv. may permit public sector organisations

1. to charge for additional services not protected by constitutional rights,

2. to campaign for investment from the private sector,

3. to save and accrue funds for specific high cost projects.

v. shall legislate to ensure that off-shore banking facilities and other tax havens are not accessible to British businesses or foreign businesses based in Britain;

vi. may impose import or export tariffs in order to nurture the domestic economy;

vii. shall impose limits and restrictions on intellectual property rights to balance reasonable rewards for innovation without causing undue constraint on new inventions;

viii. will not impose trade sanctions against any other country or be party to any other form of economic warfare against any other nation (although individuals and businesses will be free to trade or not trade with whomever they choose).

j. Employment

The economy is absolutely dependent on people working in it, if they are at all able to do so. However, there are exceptions. Young people in education and people who have passed the age of retirement (65 years) will not be expected to work but may if they freely choose to do so. Otherwise,

i. Citizens of working age who are capable of work will be expected either to work for at least 20 hours per week helping to provide some form of recognised public service, or to work in the private sector and pay an income tax.

ii. The citizen will be entitled to work at any lawful occupation of their choosing, providing such work is available and the citizen is capable of doing it.

iii. Employers will ensure that the constitutional rights of employees are provided for.

iv. The State will otherwise ensure that any adult citizen who wants to work, and is able to do so, will be employed for a maximum of 20 hours per week helping to provide a public service. If the citizen wants to work more than 20 hours a week they will be free to do so, but the choice will be the citizen's, not the state's.

v. Citizens of working age who are able and capable of work and who are not engaged in work-related education or training, and who choose not to work for at least six months a year, will not be forced to do so, but may not be entitled to receive state benefits.

vi. People working for the state will not be required to pay income tax on payments received from the state.

k. Taxation

The State may waive the payment of income taxes by those on low incomes and or those working to provide public services. Otherwise, general principles of taxation will be as follows:

i. County councils are responsible for:

1. collection of all taxes in their areas, 10% of which total amount must be delivered to the State Treasury,

2. managing county spending according to the wishes of citizens living in that area.

ii. Income tax shall not normally exceed 10% of income for individuals and businesses (and may be less at the discretion of the relevant council for cases of particular financial difficulty). However, the top 5% of the highest individual earners and richest businesses may be taxed up to 25%.

iii. Value Added Tax (VAT) may be charged on any non-essential goods and services, but will not exceed 10% of the cost to the purchaser of those goods or services (and may be less at the discretion of the relevant council for cases of particular financial difficulty). Luxury or non-essential goods (to be defined by statute) shall incur 25% VAT.

iv. Taxpayers will have the right to choose, if they wish to do so, which public departments benefit from their tax payments.

v. The State will control international trade agreements, and legislate when appropriate for trade tariffs and duties.

vi. Legislation for raising, changing or abolishing certain other taxes may be enacted from time to time.

vii. Using off-shore banking and financial services will ordinarily be forbidden. Specific exceptions may be made on a case by case basis, at the discretion of the state, the terms of such exception to be clearly described in an authorising licence. Citizens and/or businesses using foreign or off-shore banking or financial services will comply with regulations concerning such services and will be subject to having those services inspected regularly by Bank of England officials and/or government revenue inspectors. Any information required by those inspectors will be provided within twenty four hours by the individual and/or business concerned. Failure to do so may result in the immediate sequestration by the inspectors of all the British assets of such individuals or businesses until such information is forthcoming, and or the cancellation of any licence to use off-shore services.

I. Financial Crime

Crimes committed by any individual or business in the banking, insurance or financial services industries may result in the seizure by the State of all the assets of that business and/or individual. Such individuals may also incur substantial prison sentences and be banned for life from working again in a similar capacity.

Section 7 – The Press, Media and the Arts

Purpose – To define the rights and responsibilities of the press and media broadcasters, as well as artists. The State will provide for free expression by maintaining a public information service founded on truth, humanity and the long term viability of the nation's natural ecosystems. This service should be beyond reproach in terms of providing information that is accurate, balanced and humane, and that will still be recognised as such generations afterwards. Artists should enjoy full freedom of expression without hindrance from the State, but this Constitution does not provide protection against individual claims of slander, libel, defamation or any other claim of unlawful or unconstitutional acts.

Preamble

Throughout most of Britain's history its people have been routinely misinformed and lied to by those who presumed to lead them. This was done in order to maintain the absolute control that tiny handfuls of ruthless elites exerted over the vast majority of the population. In the real democracy that this Constitution establishes it is of vital importance that the people are continually kept well-informed in order that their decision-making is invariably good and humane. State censorship of information is anathema and cannot be tolerated; and the better informed the people are the less censorship could be justified. This Section provides for all sections of the media and of artists generally to have maximum freedom of expression, whilst recognising the vital importance of ensuring that people are not knowingly misinformed about issues that matter.

    a. Rights

        i. Censorship

State imposed censorship of any form is forbidden. The State will defend the right of the press, media and artists to unrestricted freedom of expression within the constraints of subsection b below;

        ii. Freedom of Information

British media and broadcasting authorities have the right to unrestricted access to information held by public bodies (except for the personal details of individual citizens, and providing that such access does not infringe any part of this constitution); and access to all State decision-making events and processes;

        iii. Artists and those providing venues for artists to work will not require specific licensing.

b. Responsibilities

  i.   Media organisations and companies that provide information purporting to be news or of any other factual nature will be required to ensure that information is truthful, balanced and clearly differentiates between factual content and personal opinion.

  ii. These constitutional powers permitted to media, press and artists offer no protection against charges of libel, slander or other perceived violations of the law or constitutional rights. Companies and individuals will accept responsibility for their own actions, and liability for compensation for damages if appropriate. However, compensation awards for such claims shall not be excessive, and will be in proportion to the unjustified physical loss, damage or harm actually sustained.

  iii.   The State media has the same entertainment rights as any other broadcaster, but with the additional responsibility of ensuring that its coverage of political events is founded on compassion for humanity and all other living creatures, and concern for the long term sustainability of all the world's ecosystems. Public information financed by the State shall conform to the highest standards of accuracy and humanity, and shall reflect and give equal weight to conflicting points of view. Factual information provided to the public by the State will aspire to be recognised as being beyond reproach in terms of accuracy and humanity, not only by contemporary generations, but also by the historians of generations to come.

iv. Individuals working in the news media will be personally responsible for ensuring their work conforms to the highest possible standards of honesty and humanity and never knowingly or negligently misleads or misinforms anyone.

Section 8 – The Environment and Animal Welfare, National Heritage, Agriculture, Transport, Essential Services, Communications and Natural Resources.

Purpose – To provide for the care and protection of all animals; and the preservation and proper management of national parks and places of natural and historical significance; to preserve cultural traditions, languages and customs; to ensure that Britain is capable of feeding itself, but without necessarily requiring it to do so; that affordable, efficient and reliable transport and telecommunications are maintained. This section also aims to ensure the consumption of renewable resources does not exceed the rate they are replenished, and that energy supplies are efficient, affordable and largely harmless to people, animals and the environment.

Preamble

Until quite recent times Britain's natural environment included vast forests, wetlands and seas that were home to a multitude of wild animals, birds and fishes. Almost all of it was destroyed to pander in one way or another to the greed of the super-rich. Their ridiculous economic policy of infinite growth out of finite resources is obviously unsustainable.

a. National parks, endangered wildlife, agricultural land and places of natural and historical significance will be defined by statute, and preserved, protected from harm or conserved.

b.   Cruel or negligent treatment of animals by humans will be specifically outlawed by statute and or considered a violation of this constitution.

c.   The State will ensure that agricultural land and agricultural services are sufficient to feed the population, and that sufficient reserves of vegan food are maintained such that the population could be healthily fed for at least one year in the event of a national emergency.

d.   All counties shall be required to provide and enforce legislation protecting the environment from manmade damage and pollution, and ensuring that renewable resources are not consumed at a rate greater than they are replaced.

e.   Local traditions, languages and customs may be protected by statute providing they do not conflict with these constitutional rights.

f.   Water supplies, essential services and other natural resources may be defined and protected by statute to ensure they are not exhausted at the expense of future generations. Policies encouraging the use of renewable energy sources will be supported in preference to those requiring fossil fuels.

g.   The   State   has   overall   responsibility   for
maintaining   an   efficient   public   transport   and
telecommunications system, with counties individually
responsible   for   general   administration   and
maintenance of these services in their areas.

h.   The State will ensure that no citizen is denied
access to secure shelter, food and clean water, basic
energy   supplies,   communications,   and   public
transport.

i.   Each county will ensure that villages, towns and
cities   have   public   parks   and   or   green   spaces
managed such that citizens may use them freely and
safely for rest, recreation, and public assembly and
that naturally occurring fauna and flora can thrive –
such parks or green spaces to be in sufficient size
and number they are not normally overcrowded with
people.

j.   The protections relating to this Section may not be
changed without ballots attracting 67% support from
counties   that   would   be   specifically   affected   by
proposed changes.

k.   Each county shall establish and maintain a Public
Works Department whose purpose will be maintain,
administer and coordinate the labour requirements of
all   public   services   in   that   county;   and   to   help,   if
required,   to   coordinate   any   construction   or

maintenance work being done on any public land or buildings, or public roads, railways, waterways, stations, airports and harbours, or public utilities such as communications, energy supplies and waterworks, or any other construction or maintenance work required for providing any necessary public service.

Section 9 – Social Welfare

Purpose – To define the rights and responsibilities of both the State and the citizen with regard to social welfare. No citizen shall be without food and potable water, footwear, clothing, secure and comfortable shelter and access to basic medical care, unless they choose to be without them.

The section on communes described below proposes that initially communes comprise the locations for the provision of most public services. For historical reasons, these are relatively small compared with sites providing for the private sector. However, as the role of the state grows in comparison to the role of the private sector, it may be more practical for the private sector to be located in relatively small communes, rather than the public sector.

Counties are individually responsible for containing social spending within the limits of their budgets, whilst providing for:

a.   ensuring that no child or citizen is without good footwear and clothing, secure and comfortable shelter, nourishing food, facilities for maintaining personal hygiene, and basic health care.

i. Citizens permanently needing such support from the State will permanently receive it;

ii. The State shall establish and maintain sheltered accommodation centres where the basic material provisions of this section may be supplied directly to those citizens who need them;

iii. Citizens of working age who are normally able to work will accept that State support is intended only for temporary use, and that if such citizens require State support they will comply with State support services' efforts to restore them to independent living;

iv. Any claim by the citizen of working age to the social rights described in this section are dependent on their acceptance of a duty to work for a maximum of twenty hours per week, if capable of doing so – such work to be provided by the State if necessary.

b.   paying unemployment, sickness, disability, maternity benefits and retirement pensions, as well as providing social care and emergency services. However, citizens of working age who are able to work will recognise their duty to do so.

c.   managing their own systems for punishment and rehabilitation of offenders.

    i.   Prison facilities must adequately remove persistent criminals from the law abiding community;

    ii.   The rights of convicted criminals will always be secondary in consideration to the victims of their crimes;

    iii.   Rehabilitation services will be prioritised to help criminals who sincerely accept responsibility for their crimes and have a genuine intention to reform their behaviour.

d.   protecting employment rights.

    i.   Standard minimum employment rights shall be protected by statute and or this constitution, and assumed in all cases where employers fail to provide contracts which comply with State minima.

e. communes.

Communes will provide the physical and administrative location for all public services in their area. Each county will establish and maintain communes with the following basic principles:

i. The commune will be managed by a supervisor, who shall be a resident elected by citizens living and working there, and run according to its own operating constitution, which shall not conflict in substance with this constitution;

ii. The supervisor will normally serve for one year and then stand down for a new supervisor to be elected. A supervisor may serve more than one term, but may not serve consecutive appointments;

iii. A state administrator will be appointed to serve the commune by working with the supervisor to ensure conformity with this constitution and to provide liaison with the wider state;

iv. The commune may organise itself and its workers in any lawful manner, but all work is to be equally valued and remunerated according to the Lateral Administration Model (Addendum C);

v. The commune shall try to pay its own way, but may apply for, and receive when necessary, state assistance to do so. No one person shall significantly profit financially from the commune, with any income generated being returned to the commune;

vi. People using the commune will be either resident or non-resident. All of these people shall have a right to use all the facilities of the commune providing they adhere to its rules;

vii. The commune will provide any resident or non-resident with the basic necessities stipulated in this constitution;

viii. Non-residents may have full access to the commune facilities providing they work for the commune for up to twenty hours a week in whatever capacity the managing team of the commune decides;

ix. Any citizen will have the right to live in a commune, but if they are of working age they shall commit to working up to twenty hours a week in whatever capacity the commune decides – such work to be within the citizen's capabilities;

x. No citizen will have to work for the commune for more than twenty hours a week, but may do so if work is available there and if the citizen wants to do it;

xi. Citizens living and working in the commune may also work outside it if they choose to do so, but the work of the commune shall take priority on their time;

xii. Children, people with serious disabilities and retired people living in a commune may work if they freely choose, but shall not be required to do so.

Section 10 - International Relations

Purpose - To ensure that Britain behaves as an exemplar nation in all its dealings with other countries: actively promoting peace, happiness and justice for all; actively resisting anti-democratic practices by foreign dictators and big business; actively taking part in international organisations whose purpose is to promote international peace, justice, humanity and the long-term protection of our planet and its wildlife; actively ensuring it promotes long-term sustainable living practices.

Preamble

For hundreds of years Britain's international behaviour has been similar to that of pirates and gangsters, but on a global scale. Although Britain was far from being the only country that behaved in this way, it is obviously not the way an enlightened country should conduct itself.

This section aims to provide an outline of how Britain should conduct itself as an equal partner with other nations, and as a responsible caretaker of our planet.

    a. Britain will not:

        i. take part in armed conflicts in other countries, unless acting as part of an international force on the specific authority of the General Assembly of the United Nations;

ii. provoke, initiate or encourage individuals, groups or organisations to wage armed conflicts in other countries;

iii. engage in economic warfare of any kind (such as imposing trade sanctions) on any country.

b. Britain will always behave like a good neighbour to all countries, helping others as much as possible and in full compliance with this constitution, whenever asked to do so.

c. The Department of Foreign Affairs (DFA) will be responsible for representing Britain in all its dealings with other countries. The Department will:

i. provide communication links with the governments of other countries;

ii. negotiate agreements-in-principle on behalf of the British people with the governments of other countries;

iii. refer any such agreements to the British people for formal completion and ratification;

iv. provide representation at international governmental organisations, such as the United Nations, and at other international organisations committed to promoting the values of this constitution;

v. ensure its representatives living and working in foreign countries respect and abide by the laws of those countries.

d. The DFA will not secretly or intrusively spy on other nations, only collecting and distributing information that's otherwise publicly available in that country.

e. The DFA and its representatives will not interfere in any way with the government of other countries, and will not be party to any secret plotting or acts of political violence in any other country.

f. Excepting for the personal details of individuals, all DFA information will be open, transparent and freely available to any British citizen.

g. The DFA will, through its overseas offices, provide appropriate help and support whenever necessary to any British citizen travelling in foreign countries.

Section 11 – States of Emergency

Purpose – To provide contingency arrangements for times of war[6] or natural disaster.

Preamble

In the past Britain has sometimes declared States of Emergency that have been used as a cynical device to cruelly oppress British people. This cannot be tolerated. A state of emergency can be said to exist only when some natural disaster has catastrophically effected the whole country or some significant part of it; or when the country is being attacked by the military forces of some other country and is in peril of being invaded and overrun by those forces.

> The president, acting on the authority of parliament, may declare a state of emergency either in a particular region, or nationally during times of war or natural disaster. A state of emergency will not be declared for longer than three months, but may be renewed by the support of a majority of parliamentary MPs. Decision-making may be devolved to elected councillors and MPs from the relevant areas for the duration of the declared state of emergency; but such decisions will be identified as a state of emergency decision and be valid only for the duration of the state of emergency.

The military and or police will never under any circumstances assume command over the nation's elected representatives, but may advise those representatives, when asked to do so, during the course of the emergency.

States of emergency may result in temporary suspension of the citizen's right to control the decision-making process. But such suspensions may only be justified when essential communications are not working correctly, and may only last until communications are working normally once more. A state of emergency will not affect any of the citizen's other basic rights or duties as described in Section Two and Section Three above.

Notes

1.   **Citizen** - For the purposes of this document a citizen is anyone who is:

> a. born in Britain or
>
> b. born elsewhere but is normally resident in Britain and has regularly worked in British public services or paid British income taxes for at least five years.

2.   **State** - The State is the collective term applied to the people and offices of public administration. Any person or office mainly employed to perform a public service and who receives funding from local or national treasuries for that service is a part of the State.

3.   **Britain** - The area contained within the internationally recognised territorial limits of the United Kingdom.

4.   **Properly informed** – It is the responsibility of the state to ensure that Proper Information is freely available and easily accessible to the citizen; but it is the responsibility of the citizen to access that information. Proper Information is that which provides a balance of factual, verifiable information together with the opinions of those who support and oppose any particular position, with equal time and space provided for both sides of the debate. Specialists providing information should be those who do not stand to gain personally from the outcome of a debate, and the people should always be mindful of this condition and always question the motives of

the person informing them. In addition, where relevant, Proper Information must ensure that at least half of any argument is expressed through the ethical considerations that inform this constitution and/or Ethical Guide (Addendum A).

5.   **Statistically valid sample** - A group of 100 citizens randomly selected according to standards stipulated by the National Statistics Office, and who have voting rights in the area where the sample applies.

6.   **Times of war or temporary states of emergency** – For the purposes of this clause, the meaning of "war" should be specific to the invasion of foreign armed forces within the territorial boundaries of Britain. Temporary states of emergency should be declared only when a natural disaster has destroyed the normal means of communication upon which the proper administration of this constitution depends, and applied only to areas directly affected by that loss of communication, and last only for the duration of that loss of communication. Suspension of constitutional rights is never to be undertaken lightly and should never exceed the duration of a specific national or regional emergency.

Addendum A

Ethical Guide

Purpose: The People's Constitution accepts the right of any person to practice the religion of their choice, and to peacefully practice the customs and rituals of any religion, providing such practice does not infringe this constitution. Apart from having the same rights and duties as any other citizen, no religious leader shall be permitted to have any other constitutional role in the government of the country. Therefore in the absence in the British State of any established religion, the People's Constitution promotes the following ethical guidance.

The first premise of this guide is that the existence of God (or gods) has never been proven, and until such proof is forthcoming it must be the duty of ordinary mortals to establish for themselves a humane and compassionate code for their own existence, how they interact with all living things, and for the long term viability of all living things on our planet. The core assumptions of this guide are that the purpose of human existence is the pursuit of happiness, which can only be found in helping to provide happiness for others, extending compassion to all living creatures; and in preserving our environment and natural resources for the benefit and happiness of future generations. No one should define someone else's happiness, nor hinder their search for it, providing that search does not cause suffering to other living creatures, deny the happiness of others, or cause harm to the environment, or other people's property.

These articles are not, of themselves, enforceable in law. They are standards of right and wrong to which every citizen should voluntarily adhere in order to facilitate peaceful co-existence with each other, and with all living creatures.

1. No one should kill another person.

Although the stricture that we should not take the lives of others is probably as old as human society itself, there has possibly never been a period in history where the taking of life has not been legitimised by some war or another; or assumed by the state in the shape of lawful executions. Although a very few of these wars and executions may indeed have been just, their number is tiny relative to the far greater number of unjust wars and executions.

Similarly, it is unlikely there are many doctors who have not at some stage hastened the death of some suffering person, or terminated an unwanted pregnancy. So clearly there are exceptional circumstances when the taking of another life might be totally justified, such as defending one's self or family against lethal attack, or ending terminal suffering, or terminating an unwanted pregnancy; but this number is so very small that the general case must be that taking another person's life is absolutely wrong.

2. No one should intentionally harm anyone or cause undue suffering to any living creature.

Exceptions are obviously similar to point 1 above.

3. Every person should try to make others happy.

It is not always possible to do this as some people have a natural disposition to be miserable and will go to extraordinary lengths to have their way. So where it is unusually difficult to please others through their own desire not to be pleased, a refusal to add to their troubles should suffice. A genuine pleasure in helping to facilitate the happiness of others whenever possible is natural to most people; it is an instinctive human characteristic that should be treasured and nurtured.

4. No one should steal.

Exceptions are obviously similar to point 1 above.

5. No one should damage the property of others.

Exceptions are obviously similar to point 1 above.

6. Every person should honour the agreements they make with others.

One of the most common sources of discontent and suffering is the failure of people to keep to agreements they freely make. Agreements should not be entered into unless there is a genuine commitment to honour them; and when there is a genuine reason for the agreement to change a real effort should be made to find an equitable solution for all parties.

7. Every person should help to preserve and protect the environment.

Nothing should be done to intentionally or negligently damage, harm or foul the flora and fauna, public facilities or others' private property; nor should any person or organisation who behaves recklessly in this regard be supported in any way.

8. Every person should treat all people with the same courtesy, respect and objectivity they would hope others would extend towards them.

We each have a right to be different, and to live our lives as we choose; but we can only claim that right for ourselves so long as our actions do not cause harm to any other person or living creature, and providing we recognise the rights of others to behave the same way.

9. Every person should not behave with careless indifference to the feelings of others, or with reckless negligence of the consequences of their actions.

All of us say and do things that occasionally hurt others in some way. It is impossible not to. The essential component of this principle is intention. If we do not intend to harm others, we should not be judged as harshly as those who do intend it, or those who do not care about the harm they cause.

10.   Every person should not be oversensitive to the words and actions of others when they clearly have not intended any harm.

This is the other side of the same coin. If someone has offended someone else but clearly did not intend to do so, or has not been recklessly negligent in their actions, then the possibility is that the person taking offence is being oversensitive to whatever it is that was said or done, and it is them that is at fault.

11.   No one should manipulate or use others to do wrong.

People who choose to live outside the law frequently use or pay others to be immoral or break the law for them. Manipulators such as these are more despicable than those they influence or use, and should always be regarded as such.

12.   Every person should take responsibility for their own actions, compensating others if their choices cause material loss or damage to others.

13.   Women should not have more than two children.

The planet has been overpopulated for many years. This is the single most important factor behind the ecological destruction of our environment. The state should make provision to ensure that any woman who wishes to have a child is able to do so, whilst also encouraging women ordinarily to have no more than two children.

14. Every person should work to the best of their ability in order to provide for themselves and their families, and to help and support wider society.

The State is obligated to help people use their labour in useful or enjoyable ways, to help provide good employment in the public services for anyone who is able to work but is struggling to find it. But the citizen should recognise the importance of willingly contributing their labour in exchange for the State's support, and understand how important their labour is to the success of society. However, no one should be compelled to spend most of their waking hours doing work they do not want to do. A certain maximum number of hours per week (20, say) should be recognised as a sufficient labour requirement to expect from a working-age adult in return for the full protection of this constitution and the State; but that maximum requirement must not be unnecessarily onerous, or used as a restriction to prevent someone from working more if they choose to do so, and must allow the citizen plentiful free time to rest or use as he or she sees fit.

Addendum B

Possible Voting Mechanism

The effective working of this Constitution is only as good as the information available to citizens upon which they may form opinions, and the voting mechanism used for decision-making. There are several conditions that must be satisfied in order for a voting mechanism to be fit for the purpose for which it is meant. It must be:

a   Simple to use

b   Inexpensive

c.   Secure

d.   Trustworthy

e.   Quick

As soon as the voter has cast her vote she should be able to verify instantly that her vote has been correctly recorded. She should be able to check at any time thereafter that her officially recorded vote is exactly the same as that verification (i.e. has not been changed).

The following simple system should provide the framework for a suitable computerised database. Each completed vote should contain the following details:

Voter Details			Vote Reference			Vote	
NINO	D.o.B	Password	Date	Debate Venue	Debate Ref.	Sheet Ref.	Detail

Voter Details

The voter inputs their personal information into the required fields: National Insurance Number (NINO); Date of Birth; Password.

Vote Reference

When the voter inputs the date, default options should appear in 'Debate venue' according to whether the debate is national, county or something else. Possible venues should be determined by the NINO, showing only those venues where the voter is eligible to vote. Once the venue is selected default options should then appear in 'Debate Ref.' according to the specific debate the voter wants to vote on.

Vote

Once the 'Debate Ref' field is selected, an alphanumeric code should appear in 'Sheet Ref'. This is the specific place where the voter's vote is recorded and stored. It is a unique two-part reference for that particular voter (e.g. sheet BX7 line 33). A dropdown menu should appear in 'Detail' where the available voting options should then appear for that particular debate.

Verification

It is essential that the voter has complete confidence that his vote is correctly counted and recorded. Although it is highly desirable that the details of a voter's choice should be secret, this is secondary in importance to the voter knowing that the details are accurately recorded and counted. (The main purpose of the secret ballot is to eliminate intimidation and/or bribery. However, it is inconceivable that the scale of bribery or intimidation required to significantly affect a public ballot could be kept secret, and as the constitution provides considerable penalties for corruption, it is unlikely to be a serious problem.)

A printed copy of the voter's choice should be instantly available as soon as all the fields have been completed.

If the voter wanted to verify that her vote had been correctly recorded on the national database, she should be able to check it without much difficulty. The following is a possible mechanism for doing so:

The voter should be able to access from any internet connection a public archive which, when she inputs details of the Debate Venue, Debate Ref. and the **first** part of her unique Sheet Ref. (BX7 in this example), a display should then reveal a whole sheet of fifty vote results, say. The sheet would show the details of those fifty votes, and the vote statistics for that sheet, but would conceal individual voter identities. The voter could check the recorded vote for line 33 without the computer knowing which result she's checking. When she then inputs her Voter Details the whole of line 33 should then be revealed confirming that it is in fact her record and no one else's, which should exactly match the printout she received after making her vote.

To check (if she wanted to) that her vote has been recorded correctly on the national result she should then be able to work upwards via the Ward Count (the statistical record of all the sheets for that debate in that ward), to the District Count (the statistical record of all the Ward Counts for that debate in that district), to the County Count (the statistical record of all the District Counts for that debate in that County), to finally the National Count. So there should be a straightforward data trail that any voter can check for themselves, if they want to do so, to see exactly how their vote has contributed to the National total.

NB. **It is essential that a 'veto' option is always included wherever it is possible to do so.** This is to protect the voter from situations where the only options presented to her to choose from are all undesirable, and where the voter's choice is best expressed by preferring to reject the proposed change altogether.

Addendum C

Organisation of Public Services

This Constitution provides for the citizen to directly control their government. This provision is not confined to only voting for representatives, it provides for the citizen to have significant control over their public services too. The citizen controls how public services are financed – either by authorising (or not authorising) the state to provide finances for any particular public service; or (in the case of taxpayers) choosing how their taxes are apportioned.

This could be achieved through two related mechanisms.

1. The citizen is invited, but not compelled, to vote for the authorisation of finances to particular public services - or to provide an annual statement choosing which public services should benefit from his taxes, and by what proportions.

2. In this Constitution all public services are organised entirely differently to the traditional hierarchical system. They employ a lateral administration model:

Lateral Administration Model

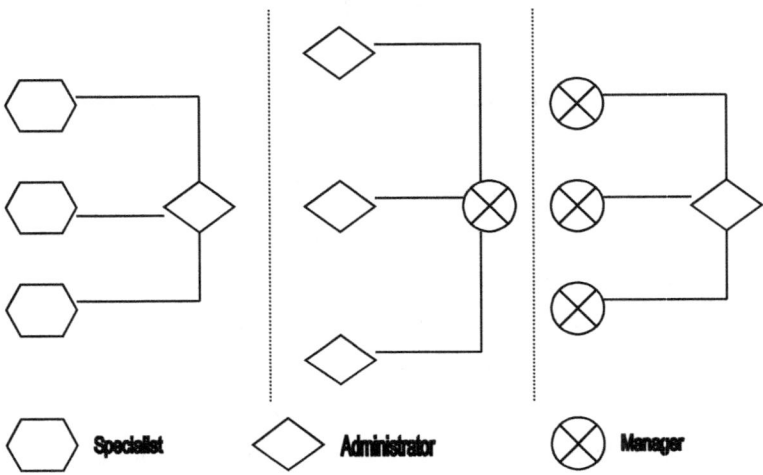

○ Specialist ◇ Administrator ⊗ Manager

In this model the specialist is usually anyone who directly provides a public service. It is usually the person who personally deals directly with the public, and could be anyone such as a policeman, teacher, clerk or nurse, say; but may also be professional people such as accountants, lawyers and engineers whose personal contact with the public might be limited. The activities of the specialists are coordinated by a manager, whilst the administrative support links between managers and specialists are provided by administrators. It is a system of equals, where everyone doing similar work is paid the same and receives the same conditions of service, and where none are more important than any other or have greater authority than any other. Managers appoint and may dismiss specialists and administrators, and are themselves elected by those they will manage; but are officially appointed by, and may be dismissed by, elected councillors.

These two mechanisms combine together in the Public Sector Accountability Model, and show how much influence the citizen has in the delivery of public services. Here, the citizen can influence the amount of treasury budget that's received by a particular public service, and can, in addition to dealing directly with the manager of the service being provided, also appoint, and recall (dismiss) the councillor who is responsible for that manager. The diagram below shows the lines of control: the citizen "customer", has direct influence of the two main controls of any public service department, the treasury and councillors, and therefore has significant control of the department itself.

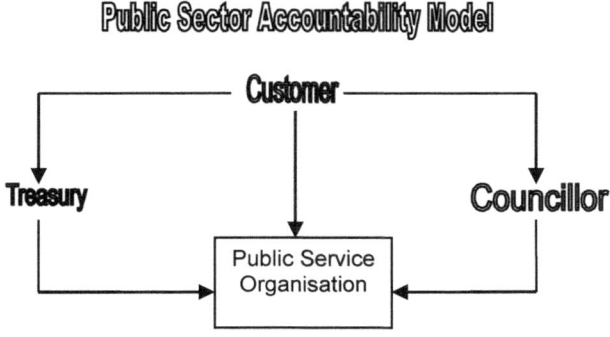

About the Writer

John and Lorraine at "Castaways" Beach Rarotonga February 2004

John was born in Bournemouth in 1954. His parents, having lived in South Africa and Southern Rhodesia since the end of World War Two, and returned to England so John could be born there, decided to go back to Africa again almost as soon as John appeared. The little family lived in Kenya,

Uganda and Northern Rhodesia before eventually settling in Bulawayo back in Southern Rhodesia in 1958.

John was educated at Baines Primary and Junior Schools in Bulawayo, Hatfield Junior School during a short period when the family lived in Salisbury (during which time UDI was declared), and Milton High School upon returning to Bulawayo at the start of 1967. John was a very average scholar, seldom exerting himself to do anything more than was absolutely necessary, and excelling only in the number of beatings he received for various minor disciplinary offences. He never thought of school (which he usually called "prison") as anything other than an irritating interruption to his freedom, which he always prized.

Even as a very small child he was not much good at following people he did not trust or like, and has always been instinctively suspicious of authority. Neither was he ever seized with a strong desire that others should follow or copy him, and has never been comfortable telling people what to do. He was always mystified why people should not be left alone to make their own choices, instead of having to be led, or told what to do all the time.

On leaving school he began what was to become a fairly itinerant employment record, working firstly for the Standard Bank at Belmont in Bulawayo, and then the Ministry of Internal Affairs, where he was posted to Plumtree and then Filabusi. John was sacked from that job for being absent without leave whilst doing national service with the department. After successfully evading for a couple of years call up for national service in the army, he eventually submitted to the inevitable and joined the army as a regular soldier in 1976.

Passing an officers selection board he trained at the School of Infantry in Gwelo for about nine months, but was expelled from the course for lack of enthusiasm following the capitulation of the Ian Smith government resulting, as John and many others saw it, in a situation where there was even less point in being shot than had previously existed.

John worked for a year for Rhodesia Railways as a station foreman, based at Serule in Botswana, saving money in order to try to pursue the only career ambition he ever had – studying medicine.

He left his beloved Rhodesia for good in 1979 shortly before it became Zimbabwe, fetching up in Grantham in England, where his parents had settled a year previously. After studying for two years John obtained reasonably good 'A' levels and was accepted into St Mary's Medical School in Paddington. However, he failed his first year exams and had to leave.

John worked for a couple of years in various children's homes, a job he enjoyed, but was sacked in 1986 after writing a controversial article in a national social work magazine, his first personal encounter with Britain's hypocritical posture as world exponents of "free expression".

Over the years, as life gradually produced more and more confirmation for his prejudices against authority, he became even less tractable, and progressively more appalled with the brutal injustice of society, and the corruption, negligence and sheer evil of the world's leaders.

His dismissal for writing a controversial article proved to be the start of John's writing career and political activism. He set-to writing his first novel, *"Come the Revolution"*, which was also the first primitive statement of the very same principles laid out in this book. Although the book was completed around 1986, he could not find a publisher for it – a situation which would become monotonously familiar.

A period of stability began in 1988 when he passed the civil service exams for executive officers, and joined the Employment Service in November that year.

On 11th August 1994, Julie, John's first wife, a beautiful, fragile person, died from cystic fibrosis. They had been married for ten years.

John's civil service career came to an end in April 2003. Furious with Tony Blair's decision to join the illegal American adventure in Iraq, he resigned his safe and cushy job to create his own political party, The Organisation of Free Democrats, and set about trying to change the world. The first edition of *"Free Democracy"*, the forerunner of this book and little more than a pamphlet, was produced in 2005; and a second novel, *"The Chartist"*, later changed to *"The Road to Emily Bay"*, came the following year. Acknowledging that fiction was not his forte, John settled to writing political essays and radical pamphlets, which is far better suited to his abilities. In addition to almost yearly updates of this book, John started producing *"The Edge"* in 2007, a dissident monthly pamphlet; but with negligible distribution and lack of funds it folded about a year later.

The Organisation of Free Democrats dissociated itself as a political party in 2008 (but continued as a website - where this constitution was freely available to anyone who wished to use it - until it was killed-off in a cyber-attack in 2015). The scrapping of Free Democrats as a political party was due to a growing realisation that party politics are the real cancer of democracy, and that a formal political party was not only irrelevant to the aims of Free Democracy, it was hypocritical too. John has tested the principles of this constitution six times in the Grantham area by competing in elections: the general election in 2005 and local elections in 2007, 2009, 2011, 2013 and 2015. Although he has not yet won a poll, he did win one vote in three in 2011, and one in four in 2015 – remarkable outcomes for such a radical platform.

John was also briefly a member of the Green Party between 2013 and 2015. Discovering that the Greens' policies were almost identical to this Constitution John and Lorraine tried to make them reality through the Greens. However, upon discovering that the Greens are not truly committed to their own policies (as evidenced by their disastrous 2015 election campaign), they both quit the Party in May of that year. They both joined the Labour Party when Jeremy Corbyn was elected leader, but left about a year later on making two important discoveries: unlike the Greens, Labour has no basic policies, no core identity; and it is terribly split, with a vicious and powerful right-wing component. John and Lorraine re-joined the Greens.

John and Lorraine were married on a beach on Rarotonga, Cook Islands, in 2004. She supports all his efforts with a loyalty, commitment and devotion he knows he can never repay; and he wholeheartedly accepts that this book owes at least as much to Lorraine for its existence as it does to him. Indeed, it is as much a product of their union as any child, and a permanent legacy to both of them.

They live a very happy vegan anarchist lifestyle together in Great Gonerby, England.

www.ingramcontent.com/pod-product-compliance
Lightning Source LLC
Chambersburg PA
CBHW071424180526
45170CB00001B/210